"There is scarcely a house in the village that has not had the help and the comfort of their ministrations, and they have gone into all the surrounding sections and even to considerable distances."

JOHN KING LORD, L.L.D.

The Mary Hitchcock Memorial Hospital
Its First Quarter Century
1919

Hiram Hitchcock's Legacy

Hiram Hitchcock's Legacy

the history of the
Mary Hitchcock Memorial Hospital
School of Nursing

Loretta Churney Land, R.N.

Published for the
MARY HITCHCOCK MEMORIAL HOSPITAL
by
PHOENIX PUBLISHING
Canaan, New Hampshire

Land, Loretta C
Hiram Hitchcock's legacy.

Bibliography: p. 138
Includes index.
1. Mary Hitchcock Memorial Hospital, Hanover, N. H.
School of Nursing—History. I. Title.
RT80.N42H364 610.73'07'117423 80-13044
ISBN 0-914016-66-0

Printed in the United States of America
by Courier Printing Company
Binding by New Hampshire Bindery
Design by A. L. Morris

Hiram Hitchcock

It was Mr. Hitchcock's wish that the activities of the institution should include a provision for the training of nurses, and accordingly a school for this purpose was set up immediately upon the opening of the Hospital.

Leon B. Richardson
Fifty Years of Service
a History of the Mary Hitchcock Hospital
1893 - 1943

Acknowledgments

I am grateful to those persons who answered the questionnaires, letters, and surveys, as well as those who were interviewed or participated in this project in any way. It is impossible to mention each by name but I would like especially to thank the members of the Advisory Committee, particularly Susan Henderson who wrote the original project proposal, and Hilda Batchelder and Marilyn P. Prouty who also supported my early efforts to initate this work. In addition appreciation should be expressed to Patricia Elder and the staff of the Mary Hitchcock Memorial Hospital Information Services; Frances Gibney, Marguerite Hastings and the staff of the New Hampshire Board of Nursing Education and Nurse Registration; Virginia Parker, Caroline Shearman, Aagot Wright, Walter Wright, and the staff of the Special Collections Department of Baker Library.

L.C.L.

CONTENTS

Advisory Committee	viii
Foreword	ix
Prologue	1
Part 1 / Beginnings	
The Early Days	7
Expansion	17
Nursing Is Organized	28
Nursing in World War I	33
Part 2 / Growth	
Postwar Adjustment	41
Student Life	52
The Depression Years	60
The Students	70
Nursing in World War II	75
Students and the War	84
Part 3 / Maturity	
A Time of Change	91
An Expanded Role	112
Epilogue	127
Appendices	
Curriculum	133
Bibliography	138
Alumnae Association	141
List of Illustrations	142
Index	144

Advisory Committee

John W. Hennessey, Jr.
President, Mary Hitchcock Memorial Hospital
Board of Trustees

James W. Varnum
Executive Director, Mary Hitchcock Memorial Hospital
Vice President, Dartmouth-Hitchcock Medical Center

Marilyn P. Prouty, R.N.
Administrator/Nursing
Mary Hitchcock Memorial Hospital

Hilda Batchelder, R.N.
Director
Mary Hitchcock Memorial Hospital School of Nursing

Dora Jane Johnson, R.N.
Alumni Association
Mary Hitchcock Memorial Hospital School of Nursing

Alice Straw, R.N.
Alumni Association
Mary Hitchcock Memorial Hospital School of Nursing

Susan J. Henderson, R.N.
Instructor
Mary Hitchcock Memorial Hospital School of Nursing

Roberta Miller
Senior Nursing Student
Mary Hitchcock Memorial Hospital School of Nursing

William L. Wilson
Retired Executive Director
Mary Hitchcock Memorial Hospital

FOREWORD

IN 1980, the Mary Hitchcock Memorial Hospital School of Nursing closed after eighty-seven years of preparing students for practice as R.N.'s. In reflecting about this event, one cannot help but look over its history. In so doing, it is evident that it parallels the history of other nursing schools which were founded and supported by hospitals in the United States. The women, and later men, enrolled in the schools provided the nursing care of patients in the hospital and, to some extent, in the community. Since 1893, the year of the school's founding, the school has continually responded to changes in health care, education and society. Once again the school is responding to changes in nursing education in closing the diploma program and opening the way for another kind of nursing education.

Like many other diploma schools of nursing, no history of the school had been written. In order to preserve the contribution of Mary Hitchcock Memorial Hospital School of Nursing to the history of professional nursing in the United States, this seemed to be an appropriate time to publish the history. A project proposal was written by Susan Henderson, an instructor in the school. She noted that, "Lack of adequate documentation and preservation of historical records within most schools of nursing is a handicap faced by all researchers of nursing history . . . The past has much to offer. Its value lies in providing us with a basis upon which to plan for the future, rather than leaving the future to intuition and chance."

Loretta Churney Land, a former instructor in the school, was designated to research and write this history. She used school and hospital records, conducted surveys, and interviewed graduates, former directors of the school and other people closely associated with the school in her effort to document its evolution. Educational, political and social trends as well as developments in health care which influenced changes in the school are documented and presented in an interesting, readable manner.

This book will not only serve as a resource, but it also enables the school to close with dignity and with the assurance that its significant contribution to the development of nursing education and to the health care of people in the Upper Valley, as well as elsewhere, has been recorded and preserved.

Marilyn P. Prouty, R.N.
Administrator/Nursing
Mary Hitchcock Memorial Hospital

Hilda Batchelder, R.N.
Director
Mary Hitchcock Memorial Hospital
School of Nursing

Hanover, New Hampshire
November 9, 1979

Hiram Hitchcock's Legacy

Prologue

LIFE IN NEW ENGLAND was difficult for the early settlers. Cold winters, thin rocky soil, and severe illness threatened their existence. An early account of the Pilgrims' first winter refers to persons chosen because of their skill to care for the sick. Duties for these male and female "nurses" included gathering wood and maintaining fires, bathing and feeding the ill, general household work, and ". . . all ye homely and necessaire offices for them wich dainty and quesie stomacks cannot endure to hear named . . ."

When the American Revolution broke out in 1775 the thermometer was in use and blood pressure could be measured. Bacterial infection was not yet understood, therefore asepsis was not practiced. With no anesthesia surgery was rarely performed. Some measure of relief could be given to the unfortunate amputee victim by means of opium, whiskey, or rum. The few hospitals also served as almshouses in some towns, and none had any trained nurses.

With the advent of the war some women were employed to care for the sick and wounded. These "nurses" performed general housekeeping duties and kept the soldiers as comfortable, clean, and well-fed as possible. Because of meager food, scant clothing, and poor sanitation there were high incidences of disease. Cholera, dysentery, and pneumonia were rampant. Although these women were not trained in the art of nursing, they served a great need.

Following the Revolution there were still only a few hospitals in the country (perhaps nine), and they were used to shelter the poor and the criminals as well as care for the sick. Women engaged in nursing at this time were looked upon with suspicion. In the public's opinion nursing was considered the lowest work and the moral character of a nurse questionable. In some city hospitals nursing duties were performed by elderly female inmates from the jail. In general, hospitals were deplorable places and the nurses were usually women who could get no other work. The exceptions were the hospitals run by the religious orders. Here the nursing was good and the members of the orders dedicated and educated.

The late eighteenth and early nineteenth centuries saw the rapid growth of the United States. The Industrial Revolution brought thousands of immigrants each year, and as the country grew hospitals were built and the need for nurses increased. Various hospitals lay claim to having the first school for nurses. The significance here is that several persons saw the need for some type of training for nurses and attempted it. Lectures and short courses in nursing were offered in a few places and some physicians tutored nurses. By 1861 there were about sixty-eight hospitals in the country.

At the start of the Civil War most nursing was still done by the religious orders. Now more help was needed. An appeal brought forth hundreds of volunteers and more than two thousand women from north and south served as nurses during the war. Approximately one hundred were given a month's training in order to act as supervisors and chief nurses for the Union armies. Although duties of the nurses were similiar to those in the Revolutionary War eighty-six years before, medicine was advancing. Ether had been discovered and the hypodermic syringe recently invented.

After the Civil War modern nursing evolved quickly. The first three American schools based on the Nightingale plan* were established in 1873. The early programs called for a twelve month period of study, and later this was increased to twenty-four. The first nursing manual was published in 1879 by a committee of doctors and nurses and another text on nursing appeared in 1885. As hospitals were built more schools of nursing came into existence. In 1883 the country had twenty-two schools of nursing; this number multiplied by ten in only thirteen years. Thereafter an explosion occurred and schools of nursing sprang up all over the country at an astonishing rate. Many schools set and maintained high standards for nursing; others recruited anyone who would work as a student.

* Florence Nightingale (1820-1910) was the person most responsible for the development of modern nursing. As a well-bred young woman of English society, she divorced convention and dedicated her life to the profession. Her outstanding work reformed nursing as her ideas and writings reached far beyond the British Empire. Nursing today owes its foundation to this extraordinary woman.

The term "trained nurse" had taken on a nebulous meaning, and nurses themselves were concerned. There were no standards for nursing practice or nursing education and since they varied from school to school, so did the nurses. Unsure of their co-workers' credentials, nurses were wary and skeptical. There was little in the way of sharing or communication between the schools of that day, although an attempt was made in the early journals to provide for this communication. In addition the public had no protection from poorly trained nurses. All too many citizens had experienced, or heard of trained nurses who knew little about the care of the sick.

The need for organization and standardization of nursing and nursing education was pressing. In 1893 nurses from all over the United States met at the Chicago World's Fair to consider the problems and status of the profession. This landmark meeting set off the great task of uniting nurses throughout the country and laying the foundation for the changes to come.

Into this uncertain atmosphere the Mary Hitchcock Memorial Hospital Training School for Nurses was born.

Part 1

Beginnings

1

The Early Days

DURING THE FINAL DECADE of the nineteenth century nursing leaders began organizing their profession. Schools were developed and attempts made to set and maintain standards. As nursing education gradually improved, the image of the trained nurse changed. The public began to see a skilled and conscientious individual capable of rendering dependable care.

Medicine was also progressing. The science of bacteriology enabled physicians to understand the causes of certain illnesses as well as perform more sophisticated surgeries. Many exciting discoveries were being made and for the first time health care was based on scientific principles.

It was another matter, however, to get this information and care to the public. People were slow to accept this new type of medicine in place of the familiar "Beecham's Pills," "Johnson's Anodyne Liniment" (for internal or external use), "Dr. Baker's Grape Cure," or "Dr. Pierce's Golden Medical Discovery."

Hiram Hitchcock and his wife Mary came to Hanover, New Hampshire, from New York around 1870. Mr. Hitchcock was a man of diverse interests and he and Mrs. Hitchcock were soon part of this small New England town. They were known and respected in the community and Mr. Hitchcock became an active, prominent citizen. In 1887 Mrs. Hitchcock died and two years later Mr. Hitchcock announced his plans for a memorial to his beloved Mary: A hospital bearing her name.

There was no hospital in Hanover at that time. Early establishments for this purpose had been privately owned, or temporary in nature. Dr. Dixi Crosby had maintained a small hospital on College Street, but it had not been in operation after his retirement in 1870. Therefore a tract of land in the northern sector of the town was secured, a charter obtained, and foundations laid. Construction

The Mary Hitchcock Memorial Hospital shortly after completion in 1893 with the rolling hills of Hanover beyond.

began and four years later the building was completed. The entire project was paid for by Mr. Hitchcock, it being understood that upon completion of the facility the community would absorb the cost of its administration and maintenance.

Many citizens were skeptical. Thirty-six beds seemed excessive and worse still there would be the expense of running such an institution! Could the community afford it? There was also a certain amount of fear regarding hospitals — after all, people often went there and died! The citizens of Hanover had survived all this time without a hospital, was one necessary now?

Others were pleased and impressed with such a large and modern facility. No detail had been overlooked. There were comfortable private rooms and wards, a kitchen, laundry, heating plant, and an operating theatre. Operations would now be performed in the hospital instead of on kitchen tables. The new building also had gas and electricity. In addition physicians at the Dartmouth Medical School could oversee the treatment of their patients and good nursing care would be available not only in the hospital but also in residents' homes. The hospital would provide educational opportunities for students at the medical school, and there would be a place to care for college students who became ill. To many the idea of receiving health care seemed safer now.

On May 3, 1893, the Mary Hitchcock Memorial Hospital was dedicated with appropriate public ceremonies. Fifteen days later the first patient arrived and was cared for by the hospital's two nurses. In July two young women were admitted as students of nursing and the Mary Hitchcock Memorial Hospital Training School for Nurses commenced operation.

Miss Theresa G. Leach, the hospital's first superintendent, conscientiously administrated her duties as suited her precise manner. She managed the work of the entire hospital, seeing that each part ran smoothly while conducting the education of the nursing students and overseeing the care received by patients. Her enthusiasm lent itself to the tasks at hand and John King Lord wrote of her

. . . with a gift for organization, able to direct as well as to plan, though sometimes more given to the enforcement of rules than to consider the reason for them, and occasionally laying more stress on the form than the substance, she put the new institution into working order and efficiently directed its enlarging work.

The first head nurse was Maude Hamington, whose responsibility it was to render or assign patient care and manage the hospital's nursing service as well as assist with the training of the pupil nurses.

The training school was set up as a two year course of study ". . . similar to other well conducted schools." Early records are scant, but it is possible to ascertain significant elements of nursing and nursing education at Mary Hitchcock in the 1890s.

Application to the training school was made in writing on the proper form to the Superintendent of Nurses, Miss Leach. Admission requirements dictated that the applicant be a female between twenty-one and thirty-five years of age, strong, healthy, and of good common

The handsome porch of the new facility offered a warm welcome to all who entered.

sense. A character reference was requested, and it was also felt that a nurse should be responsible, gentle, good-tempered, and able to exercise self-denial.

Students were admitted as vacancies occurred in the school. Space, hospital needs, and provisions for instruction determined how many students the training school could accommodate. It was customary that only one student entered at a time. Records indicate that as the hospital became more accepted and the number of patients increased, more students were enrolled.

Once admitted to the school, the student served a two month probationary period during which time her fitness for nursing was determined. Upon satisfactory completion of this period she became a junior, or first year nurse and she would receive a small monthly stipend to cover expenses for uniforms and books. In exchange for services to the hospital she would receive the education and training necessary for a nurse.*

The new probationer arrived at Mary Hitchcock with two or three washable dresses, several white aprons, quiet shoes, a warm wrapper, and "waterproof equipment." She was assigned a room on the third floor of the hospital where the employees also lived, and she signed an agreement to remain two years and to obey rules. After putting away her personal belongings the probationer reported for duty, was assigned to a ward, and started her training.

Patient care facilities at this time included the east and west wards, private rooms, a sunporch, a "surgery" to make up dressings and mix solutions, and a diet kitchen. Once assigned to a ward the new nurse carried trays, dusted, or performed other light housekeeping duties. Gradually she was taught basic nursing skills: bathing, feeding, and general patient care. Nursing, or practical skills, were taught on the wards by the superintendent and head nurse. In time some of this teaching was assumed by the seniors, or second year student nurses.

* After several years the probationary period became synonymous with "preliminary term". Basic theories and skills were taught as each student's aptitude for nursing was evaluated. Probationers or "probies" were easily identified by their uniforms which were a different color, composition, or material than those worn by other students. Until recent years these students often performed unskilled tasks such as carrying trays, stacking linen, mopping floors, general cleaning, and of course obeying orders from all of a higher rank. The length of the probationary period varied from time to time ranging from two to six months. At the end of the term those whose nursing care and classwork were satisfactory received the school cap while those failing to meet prescribed standards were dismissed from the school.

The winding staircase from the impressive rotunda led to the private ward on the second floor and the nurses' quarters on the third.

The superintendent, head nurse, and the students made up the entire nursing staff.

Students worked seven days a week with a half day off each week. Day duty began at 7:00 A.M. and ended at 8:00 P.M., with time off for meals and a two hour break at some time during the day. Those working the night duty went on the wards at 8:00 P.M. and remained until 7:00 A.M. New students began with day work, progressing to night duty in as few as three months. Night duty was considered part of the educational process and each nurse took her turn. In 1898 a student was found sleeping while on duty one night and was given the punishment of remaining in the training school for three months following her graduation.

Since the training school was not endowed finances were of concern from the start. The hospital was to institute a free or endowed bed system to help defray it expenses, but the nursing school received no financial aid. Therefore the paid employment of nursing students in nearby residences enabled the school to give some financial return to the hospital. This process also provided a community service.

A Wyeth-like atmosphere of simplicity characterizes this 1893 photograph of a typical private room.

During its first year of operation the average daily occupancy of the hospital was only 5.5 patients. Thus, nurses could be spared to work in private homes without weakening the hospital's nursing force. Since many families desired the services of nurses in their homes to care for the ill, nurses were soon going out on cases not only in Hanover and surrounding towns, but also as far away as Lancaster, New Hampshire.

A variety of cases and experience awaited the student nurse on private home duty: typhoid fever, grippe, fractures, peritonitis, and heart disease. Cases of Bright's Disease, confusional insanity, and childbirth were also common. A nurse never knew just what awaited her. Under a physician's direction she remained on a case as long as she was needed — one day or several weeks. As the hospital gained acceptance and more patients were admitted, nurses could not be spared. During the hospital's busiest times residents had to do without private home nursing.

Some interesting yet disconcerting circumstances were encountered. Many families kept large staffs of help, others had no servants. Private duty nursing was a twenty-four hour job, therefore how did the nurse fit into the family and household routine? If the lady of the house was ill and no servant was retained, who did the cooking and washing? When would the nurse be relieved of duties long enough to leave the sickroom? Were her meals taken with the family, alone, or with the patient? According to early documents it was expected that the nurse in the home where no servant was kept would "... be ready as far as her special duties will allow, to render any service which may be needed in the spirit of true helpfulness."

A small pamphlet was given to families and patients to explain the duties and purposes of the nurse in a home. The student brought this with her when called to a patient. It stated the name of the physician and nurse attending the ill person and listed some duties the nurse might perform and charges for services rendered. The family was expected to provide room and board for the nurse, and pay $1.00 per day for juniors and $1.50 for senior nurses. There were also weekly rates for longer cases. It was understood that a first year student could attend one-hour classes five days a week. Sometimes two nurses were on a case which might have made it easier for the nurses in terms of attending classes or having time off. Travel expenses (often by horse and buggy) were paid for by the family. Families were also instructed that the nurse was to have time away from the sickroom for rest and recreation, as well as to attend church weekly (unless the patient was extremely ill). Also if employed for several consecutive nights the nurse was to have six hours a day out of the patient's room. Finally, the brochure clearly stated that the nurse ". . . must not be expected to share the patient's bed."

Theoretical instruction as well as practical experience were included at the Mary Hitchcock Training School. In addition to nursing care and procedures, students received lessons in cooking, bandaging, and massage. Operating room drills and recitations were held and the students rotated through the operating room, assisting with surgeries. This rotation varied from student to student. It appears that while some had extended periods of operating room work, three or four months all told, those who did not have such a long term of surgical work had more private duty in area homes.

Lectures were also given by college professors and physicians. Drs. Smith, Frost, Gile, and Bartlett lectured the earliest classes on anatomy, physiology, medical and surgical disorders, and obstetrics. As new physicians came to the hospital they shared in the teaching of student nurses. Classes taught by lecturers were held two or three times a week from October through May. Examinations were given in all subjects

In 1893 the Superintendent's office sported a rolltop desk, a fireplace, and a somewhat unconventional lighting arrangement.

and it was necessary to pass these. Inability to keep up with classwork or unsatisfactory ward work could result in dismissal from the school.

Upon completion of the course of study nurses were graduated. There were no group or formal graduation exercises, and nurses left the school two years to the day after they entered, having had three weeks vacation a year and a small allowance for sick time. In the case of a longer illness the nurse remained in the school until the lost time was made up. Leaves of absence were granted for good reasons, and some students completed their training in segments. Most worked as private duty nurses, but a few obtained employment in the hospital or took positions teaching student nurses.

Miss Leach, a capable and efficient superintendent, managed the hospital and training school for the first seven years. She taught and supervised some twenty-seven pupils who graduated between 1895 and 1901. Miss Leach resigned in 1901 and was replaced briefly by Miss Jessie Glenn who had been the hospital's head nurse for five years. This same year Miss Ida Frances Shepard, a graduate of Boston City Hospital Training School, came to Hanover to assume the duties of superintendent of the Mary Hitchcock Memorial Hospital and Training School. Miss Shepard embraced the highest standards of her profession and inspired them in her students. She worked to establish and later helped coordinate early nursing legislation in New Hampshire. With a kind and dignified manner she skillfully directed the work of the Mary Hitchcock Hospital and its training school for nearly twenty-one years.

2

Expansion

EDUCATION FOR WOMEN developed slowly in the United States. Before the twentieth century few women had the opportunity even to attend high school. This fact inhibited collegiate preparation for nurses although early leaders viewed nursing as a profession meriting an academic foundation. Hospital-based schools provided a solution while nurses struggled for professional status. Even the best of these schools often put hospital need before education and the question raised in the minds of many concerned educators was: "Training or Education?"

The first college program for nursing education began in 1909 but the great majority of nurses then, and for decades to follow, were educated or "trained" in hospital schools. Many of these schools provided an excellent course of study and turned out superior nurses. However, these schools were opening at such a rapid rate that by 1920 there were three thousand throughout the country.

Medical science was becoming more ordered. Recent discoveries gave physicians new tools with which to diagnose and treat diseases while surgical procedures continued to advance. Medical schools underwent evaluation and many inferior establishments were closed. The American public was actively seeking health care and hospitals were acknowledged to be a necessity.

Growth of the Hospital

In spite of business reverses Hiram Hitchcock continued to give generous financial support to the Mary Hitchcock Memorial Hospital.

In fact he was responsible for the major contributions to that institution during its first eight years of operation. Therefore after his death in 1900 the loss of his benefaction was felt sharply, and the trustees worried about being able to keep the hospital open.

A program of economic thrift was instituted and the east and west wards were temporarily closed to save fuel. All hospital personnel helped as best they could to reduce costs, some doing the work of two

The East Ward in the very early days.

persons. The community at large, along with the medical school and the college, responded with financial aid enabling the hospital to pay its bills and remain open. Clearly Mary Hitchcock Hospital had proved its worth.

As the hospital grew in public favor its services also increased. In the earlier days most patients were admitted for surgery, but this was changing as more medical cases were being treated and women were coming to the hospital for childbirth. The number of children receiving care also increased.

The daily patient census rose causing the wards to become crowded and every bed was filled. This happened especially during the summer. One report written in 1907 refers to the use of two large tents erected on the hospital grounds to house patients. These tents held four to six cots each, and patients who might benefit from the fresh air were sheltered there. Apparently the condition of many patients improved with the move from ward to tent, and the nurses seemed to enjoy this change in routine almost as much as the patients. The tents were used for at least three summers, 1906 to 1908, from June to October.

The need for expansion was manifest but finances were a constant worry. At times it was difficult to keep the hospital open, still the community always did its share. In addition to financial support citizens gave the hospital gifts of food, clothing, bedding, books, flowers, rugs, magazines, and on occasion such treats as ice cream for the patients and nurses. The community always remembered the hospital, its patients, and the staff on Christmas too. This gracious practice of presenting such gifts to the hospital eventually resulted in a special day being set aside for the purpose. In 1914 "Donation Day" was declared and much support and interest was aroused.

Bequests and funds led to acquisition of new equipment and improvements in the physical plant. Between 1900 and 1920 many diagnostic and treatment tools were obtained. A new roof, a storage cellar to hold a year's supply of vegetables, and modernization of the diet kitchens with gas burning stoves all added to the efficiency of the hospital. In 1910 the entire operating theatre was remodeled by the addition of more working space and renovation of old quarters. Although these improvements added to hospital service, plant enlargement was needed greatly.

In 1911 the trustees announced plans to expand the hospital by adding a structure to the west wing. The two-story addition would run north and increase the capacity of the facility by two-thirds. The new wing was ready for occupation in July 1913 and housed a maternity ward, private rooms, a small ward, and a sunroom. Some of this area was intended for the care of children, and there was a large dining room in the basement. The new building was named the Dawn L. Hitchcock Wards, later known as the A and B wards.

This increased capacity created an even more urgent need for nurses. Therefore it was imperative that the training school should expand further.

The official uniform of the school (photo circa 1900) changed very little for nearly seventy years.

Superintendent, head nurse, house staff, and students in 1903.

Expansion of the Nursing School

The school had become a vital part not only of the hospital but also the community of Hanover. Citizens utilized the services of school nurses in their homes more than ever, and due to increased hospital activity their work was also in great demand there. It is interesting to note that although the training school had been in existence since the opening of the hospital it was not until 1906 that the trustees voted to authorize it. The school had operated for thirteen years without endorsement! This did not in any way jeopardize the productiveness of the school.

By 1902 there were sixteen pupils in the school and in 1903 there were twenty-one. This number of nurses presented serious housing problems and in 1904 a house was rented from a college professor to accommodate the head nurse and seven of the students. Two years later another house was leased for the same purpose, and in 1911 this latter residence was purchased from Mrs. A. A. Pike and refurbished as a temporary nurses' home.

At the time of planning the hospital expansion the trustees had seriously considered the need for a home for the nurses but the hospital's needs were deemed more pressing, and since there were not enough funds for both projects, the nurses home had to wait. The trustees did, however, stress the importance of obtaining a home for the nurses and expressed the hope that some benefactor(s) might make it possible. This aspiration was not realized until 1920 when the Billings-Lee Home for Nurses was constructed thanks to the generous gifts of the Billings and Lee families as well as other donors.*

In 1905 the decision was made to change the course of study at Mary Hitchcock to three years. This change conformed to the direction set by leaders of the progressive schools of that time, and led the way to developing a curriculum with increased theoretical content. Under the three-year program the student nurses now spent the first two years learning theory and receiving practical instruction in nursing. During the third year they began taking charge of the wards as senior nurses, and going to homes to do private nursing. A large part of the theoretical instruction was still given by physicians, but classroom teaching conducted by the nurses was increasing.

In October 1907 an exchange program was instituted with the training school at the New Hampshire State Hospital for the Insane in Concord. Nurses from each institution spent two months at the other school and hospital. It was felt that this was beneficial to all students and broadened their educational experience. Records indicate the exchange took place in this manner until around 1914, and then there is no mention of it or a similar program for several years.

The first formal graduation exercises took place on the evening of October 13, 1908, for those students who had completed the three-year course of study. This was the first time a class had been grouped together as such. The graduation was a public event, and the community responded in a warm and positive way by filling every seat of the Nathan Smith Laboratory at Dartmouth College. The graduation

* From 1893 to 1921 the Frederick Billings family of Woodstock, Vermont gave generous financial support to the hospital. These gifts were used for improvements or equipment and in 1920 the then existing fund was allotted to the construction of a nurses' home. Further gifts from the family (Mrs. Lee was Frederick Billings' daughter) enhanced the completion of the residence. Thus the facility was named the Billings-Lee House. Additional funds for the home came from gifts of John Freeman, Plainfield, New Hampshire, Mrs. Mary Frances Wood, Meriden, New Hampshire and the Womens' Club of Hanover, New Hampshire. Also individuals made small gifts over a period of several years for this purpose.

In 1910 students posed against a backdrop of the imposing operating room theatre.

program was such a success that it was repeated for several years but was later discontinued for a time.

Hospital Expansion Changes the Nursing School Program

Following the hospital expansion program the routine for most students changed somewhat. The first resident dietician who came in 1912 taught cooking to the students and relieved the superintendent and head nurse of some work. The appointment of a night supervisor in 1914 meant that clinical instruction would be possible for those students working at night. The head nurse (whose capacity was similar to that of today's daytime supervisors) and the superintendent carried the teaching responsibility for nursing courses.

Students went to work in the hospital at 7:00 A.M. after breakfasting at 6:30 A.M. Being late for breakfast in the dining room was punished by losing one's late permission for one month. After reporting for duty students prepared breakfast trays for the patients. Dishes and trays were stored on the wards, the food being cooked in the main kitchen and sent up in bulk containers to the ward kitchens. Trays were set up with linen tray cloths, napkins (as there were few paper products at this time), and silverware which the nurses had to polish once a month. A maid was employed to wash the dishes in the ward kitchen and the nurses washed them on her day off.

Bedmaking, baths, distribution of medications, dusting corridors, and cleaning utility rooms and bathrooms were all part of the nursing duties. Treatments were simple: mustard and flaxseed plasters for pneumonia or infection; cool baths for fevers; manipulation of traction or immobilization of casts for those with broken bones; and endless monitoring of vital signs. Pharmaceutical products included morphine, aspirin, phenacetin, mercury ointment (for syphilitic sores), and oil of wintergreen.

Surgical patients were given enemas and shaved by the student nurses. There was no recovery room and postoperative patients were promptly returned to the ward or private rooms for necessary nursing care. The head nurse or night supervisor was available to assist the busy student, answer questions, or offer instruction in a new situation. A third year student, a senior nurse, was in charge of each ward during the day. The nursing staff of the Mary Hitchcock Hospital consisted of the superintendent, head nurse, night supervisor, and the student nurses.

The operating room experience was still an important part of a nurse's preparation. A senior student was placed in charge there. She was responsible for sterilizing equipment, gloves, and gowns; making sponges and dressings; and keeping the room clean. She also made sure that the operating room ran smoothly. A scrub nurse, also a student, assisted the surgeon by passing instruments. When a nurse was assigned to the operating room she was on call at night for any case that might occur. She had to get up and assist at the surgery, clean the room, and return to bed, only to get up for duty the next day. It would seem that the surgeons were pleased with the work of the student nurses in the operating theatre. For most surgical procedures the observation area would be filled, and the operating physician would question the observers. On occasion, when a medical student had incorrectly answered a question, the surgeon would direct the query to the student nurse. She almost always knew the answer.

Night duty was also a vital part of a nurse's education, and most students worked the shift shortly after the two-month probation period was finished. A nurse reported for duty at 8:00 P.M. and remained on the assigned ward until 7:00 A.M. The night supervisor was available and a doctor, who was on call, slept in the hospital. Still, it

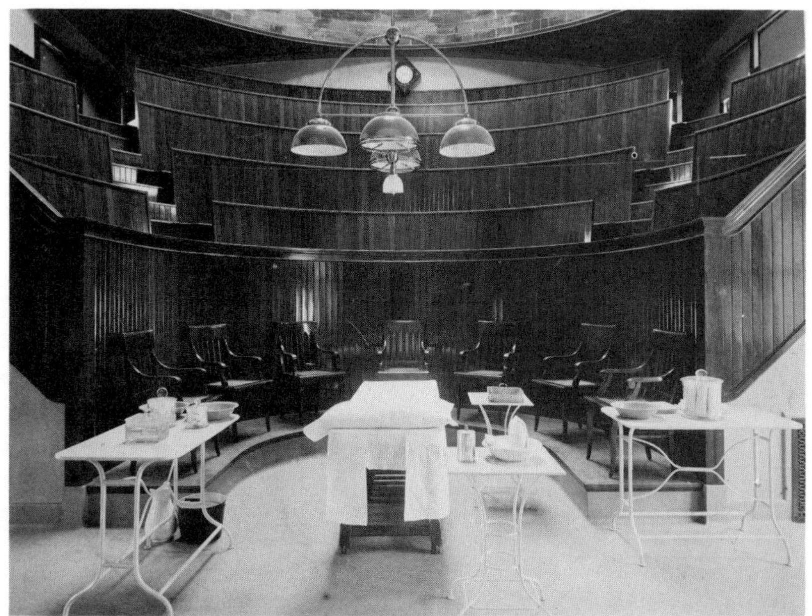

The operating room, familiar training ground for the student nurse.

could be a busy time for the student whose ward had several patients recovering from anesthesia.

In some years more young women applied to the training school for admission than could be accepted, while at other times the administration recruited nursing pupils. Often physicians would be contacted to recommend someone they knew who might be suitable for nursing.

Upon admission to the school the student served the two-month probationary period. No tuition was charged and students supplied the hospital with a dedicated and conscientious nursing staff. During the first year of school they received an allowance of eight dollars a month for books, uniforms, and other expenses. This increased to ten and twelve dollars the second and third years respectively. For many, if not most, this was the only income they had during the three years.

Student nurses were carefully watched in case unhappiness might lead to difficulty. One had to be in bed each night with lights out at 10:00 P.M. Late permission was granted once a month until 11:00 P.M., with an occasional special late permission for a dance, carnival, or other event, and such an event might warrant staying out until 2:00 A.M. Students on night duty had to be in bed by 10:00 A.M. and were

Student nurses from Mary Hitchcock and the New Hampshire State Hospital for the Insane in 1912. when a formal exchange program was in effect.

forbidden to rise before 4:00 P.M. These regulations were monitored by the supervisor or head nurse.

Students had two hours off each day and four on Sundays and holidays. A nurse could on occasion request morning or afternoon hours off in hope of using the time to her best advantage. If a class were scheduled some students might use their free time to attend. Nevertheless the young women had opportunities for hiking, picnicking, canoeing, or dancing. Several dated the young men who lived in the community or attended Dartmouth College, and a maximum amount of fun was squeezed into the little time left after studying.

Private nursing in area homes by students decreased after 1914. Records indicate that students could nurse in homes only during their third year of school, but such assignments became rare. Graduate nurses were filling this community need, but occasionally a student did private work in the hospital and slept in the patient's room on a cot.

Most significant and important at this time was the vibrant spirit of the hospital community. Physicians, nurses, and patients were a closely knit group. All were striving for the same goal—good health care—and the hospital was home for many who worked there. This dedication and spirit were especially valuable to the community when the United States entered World War I.

3

Nursing Is Organized

IT WAS A SLOW but determined effort that organized the nursing profession in the United States. Nurses joined together to promote and secure the standards that were so desperately needed. The associations they formed at local, state, and national levels facilitated their progress.

The First Nursing Associations

The American Society of Superintendents of Training Schools was founded at the Chicago Worlds Fair in 1893. This society was the first such organization for nurses in the United States. The superintendents saw the need for a similar type of association for graduate nurses and in 1897 they fostered the Nurses' Associated Alumnae of the United States and Canada. These two pioneer groups enabled nurses to consolidate their efforts to gain legislation to standardize nursing. In 1912 the Society of Superintendents became the National League of Nursing Education, and the Nurses' Associated Alumnae changed its name to the American Nurses' Association.

Training schools throughout the country formed alumnae associations and New York claimed the first statewide nurses' group. (New York was to become the national center of nursing activities as it piloted innovations and encouraged further development of the profession.)

The initial issue of the *American Journal of Nursing* appeared in October 1900 and was the first such journal to be owned and operated entirely by nurses. The magazine became the official organ of the American Nurses' Association, a function it serves today.

In 1903 four states ratified nurse practice acts and legislation governing the nursing profession took effect. Nurses throughout the country were reassured by this propitious measure. They had convinced legislators as well as the public that legal safeguards and professional standards were vital to nursing. Seventeen years later women were granted the right to vote.

With the twentieth century underway Mary Hitchcock graduates and student nurses alike closely monitored the course of national events. Their deep sense of professionalism, instilled by dedicated teachers, prompted vigorous support of the first nurse practice acts. Stimulated by the action taken in other states, they joined other nurses in New Hampshire to further the cause there.

In April 1906 fifty graduate nurses from throughout New Hampshire met in Concord to consider the formation of a state nurses' association. A second meeting in May resulted in a professional organization to be known as the Graduate Nurses of New Hampshire. Members accepted a constitution and bylaws, and an executive board was appointed. The two meetings were well attended by Mary Hitchcock graduates and Ada J. Morey, a Mary Hitchcock graduate of 1898, was elected president of the new organization, while Ida F. Shepard was elected first vice-president.

The Graduate Nurses of New Hampshire pledged themselves to work for the betterment of nursing and nursing education, to assure better health care for all, and to promote the welfare of the membership. The members also decided to affiliate with the national nurses' group, the Nurses' Associated Alumnae of the United States.

The nurses worked long and hard to promote state registration for nurses. They spent much time and effort acquainting the public with nursing issues and the importance of nursing legislation. A bill to initiate such measures was introduced in the New Hampshire Legislature and on March 7, 1907, Governor John McLane signed into law New Hampshire's first Nurse Practice Act.

A regent was appointed to oversee the implementation of the new law.* The legislation provided courses of two or more years in length (a three year waiver clause covered graduate nurses already practicing

* Two amendments to the act changed the responsibility for implementation of the law first to the Superintendent of Public Instruction, and later to the Commissioner of Education.

Alumnae from the classes of 1898 through 1909 are represented in this photograph of a reunion in the early 1900s.

and nursing students currently in schools). There was also a mandate to establish state standards for nursing schools and to appoint a board of nurse examiners to act as school inspectors. Miss Ida Shepard was named to a two-year term on this first board of nurse examiners.

Nurses immediately applied for registration. Until 1910 they could be licensed without an examination under the waiver clause. Three of the first ten certificates of registration in the state were assigned to Mary Hitchcock Memorial Hospital graduates. Certificates numbered 6, 8, and 10 were given respectively to Edna B. Snell (MHMH Class of 1905), Florence R. Fitch (MHMH Class of 1905), and Susan K. Lane (MHMH Class of 1906). Others followed and soon most of the eligible were registered. The initials R.N. began to appear in school records and Miss Shepard noted that many of the nurses in Hanover were being registered.*

* The nurses who graduated from Mary Hitchcock in 1910 were the first graduates of the school to take the State Board Examinations. Four of the seven graduating nurses took the examination in New Hampshire and were thus registered.

The Graduate Nurses of New Hampshire grew and attracted many members. The women maintained high standards for the organization, and soon a condition for membership was registration in New Hampshire. Meetings were held several times a year, and some county groups were formed. Involvement with the national association was assured by sending delegates to the national conventions. The name of the association was later changed to the New Hampshire Nurses' Association. Thanks to the endeavors of the first members, this organization was endowed with the purpose and vitality which have enabled it to grow and survive many difficult periods.

The Alumnae Association

During the two or three years spent at the Mary Hitchcock Memorial Hospital Training School, young women formed associations and friendships which often lasted a lifetime. One also felt loyalties to the school and upon graduation it was usually hard to sever ties. As the school grew the nurses began to express an interest in forming an alumnae association which would in some way help to keep the ties and be of benefit to the nurses. In the annual report of 1906 Miss Shepard noted this interest and stated the hope that a group would be initiated. However, it was to be four years until steps were taken to formally organize the alumnae.

Sixteen enthusiastic Mary Hitchcock nurses met on May 31, 1910, paid dues and became the charter members of the Mary Hitchcock Memorial Hospital Training School for Nurses Alumnae Association. Mrs. Lucia Shattuck Grey (MHMH Class of 1904) was elected president and the business of the group began.

Regular meetings were held at the school in spite of spotty attendance. (Private duty nurses had difficulty leaving their patients and distance was a problem for many.) The meetings provided companionship as well as professional enrichment. Informative programs were planned and reunions were held from time to time. The association started a newsletter thus enabling members to keep track of friends and acquaintances. Even those nurses far from Hanover had a link with the school and its alumnae.

The school itself was well served by its alumnae association. Social events were planned for the students; teas and dances proved popular. Gifts of many kinds were bestowed upon the pupils, including subscriptions to professional journals. As the years passed the alumnae group became an integral part of the training school and hospital.

Nursing Upgraded

With the advent of the Nurse Practice Act, members of the Board of Examiners worked hard to upgrade and regulate nursing education in New Hampshire. They inspected training schools and offered guidelines for improvements. Assistance was given in matters of curriculum, organization, and admission requirements, and certain textbooks were suggested for use. The nursing ideals held by these women enhanced the favorable growth of nursing in the state as they established the standards upon which the future would be built.

Early state records show that in 1911 the Mary Hitchcock Memorial Hospital Training School for Nurses began filing yearly reports with the Department of Public Instruction. The reports, first written by Miss Shepard, indicated the length of course of study, subjects taught, and the conditions of practical instruction. Names of instructors, physician lecturers, and textbooks were also included. In the earliest accounts it is notable that most of the teaching was done by Miss Shepard and the head nurse, supplemented by physicians' lectures. In 1920 there were four "instructors" to teach massage, cooking, and the nursing courses, and physicians' classes were receiving less emphasis.

In 1915 a year of high school was required for admission to the school. A year later a candidate was expected to have graduated from high school. In 1918 Miss Shepard wrote to the state ". . . We have followed the curriculum as adopted by the Board of Examiners two years ago." Clearly the nurses at the Mary Hitchcock school strove to meet and maintain prescribed standards.

4

Nursing In World War I

TODAY'S MILITARY NURSING resulted from the services of the sixteen hundred nurses who had served in the Spanish-American War. Their efforts had proven so valuable that after the war measures were taken to provide permanent nursing for the armed forces. By 1909 the Army and Navy Nurse Corps and the Red Cross Nursing Service had been established.

The United States entered World War I on April 6, 1917, and thousands of American nurses responded with a sense of duty and pride. They enrolled in the Army and Navy Nurse Corps and enlisted in the Red Cross Nursing Service. Special training camps were set up and hundreds of women entered accelerated nursing programs. As military units were shipped abroad nurses accompanied the troops to staff base camps and hospitals, and some bravely took their places in the front lines to care for the soldiers. Others remained in the United States to attend to nursing needs in military installations here. By the end of the war over twenty-four thousand nurses had served. Finally, in 1920, after much legislative discourse and overtures by nurses, the government conferred relative military rank on nurses in the armed forces.

A less obvious but no less important role in the war was fulfilled by the many nurses who were in the training schools, hospitals, and public health services of this country. These women supported the war effort by providing citizens at home with conscientious care and they maintained high standards of nursing in spite of often distressing conditions. Economic depression, lack of help, illnesses of epidemic proportions, and the uncertainty of war taxed their labors.

The Hospital in Wartime

The Mary Hitchcock Memorial Hospital felt the effects of economic decline before the United States entered the war. In 1916 supplies became very costly and at one time only ten days supply of coal was on hand. If the hospital were to remain open the management had no

A break in the day's routine, about 1918.

choice but to pay the extreme prices for food, fuel, and medical supplies. Therefore a fee was charged those patients requiring the use of the operating room, and in 1917 general hospital rates were increased.

Conditions deteriorated further as the country was drawn into the war. Supplies were not only expensive but some were difficult to obtain. The hospital was able to carry on its services, due in part to the generosity of citizens of Hanover and surrounding communities. Gifts of money, food, linens, and hospital clothing helped keep health care at a high level. The annual "Donation Day" in 1917 brought scores of friends to the hospital with vegetables, fruits, canned goods, and other items.

Although the trenches seemed far away, everyone at Mary Hitchcock felt the impact of the war. A large flag flying from the third floor of the main building was a reminder to all. The hospital itself was not used for actual war service, but a statement on file with the army outlined its capacities and resources should circumstances change. The busy surgical service was left to one physician as most of the doctors

Close friendships were formed during three years of hard work and laughter mutually shared.

were in the armed forces and stationed away from Hanover. One member of the hospital family gave his life to the cause: Dr. Henry Lee Knapp (House Officer, 1916-1917) died in France in the spring of 1918.

The Training School in Wartime

Due to wartime sentiment the Mary Hitchcock Memorial Hospital Training School for Nurses carried on in spite of increased workloads and financial hardships. The school had kept abreast of educational trends and had modified its course of study to meet state requirements as set by the Board of Examiners. Now it was one of only a few schools in the state with sufficient hospital bed capacity to meet Red Cross enrollment requirements. This afforded some advantage to the students. However, the school was unable to increase its enrollment as requested by the Council of National Defense. Lack of housing prevented expansion, but the school tried to maintain its full quota of twenty-seven nurses.

The conditions created by the war seemed to inspire students to inject more spirit and energy into their studies and hospital work. With fewer supplies and less help the nurses had to work even harder, but

The school was well represented in the Liberty Bond parade in Hanover in 1918.

the nursing care was given with the same exacting skill as always. It may have taken longer, but the work was always completed. Students pitched in and helped each other with a sense of vigor and dedication. Since each student expected to be eligible for Red Cross enrollment upon graduation, much time was spent preparing to meet the requirements.

No public graduations were held during the war. As was originally the case, each nurse simply left school when she had completed the program, and a new probationer stepped in to fill the ranks.

At Christmas in 1917, instead of the usual gift exchange among themselves, the student nurses used their money to fill thirty comfort kits for Hanover men in the service. The school's own service flag showed sixteen stars for Mary Hitchcock graduate nurses, three of whom were overseas.*

In the fall of 1918 Hanover citizens fell victim to the severe influenza epidemic. It began in mid-September and lasted nearly two months. The hospital became so crowded that beds were placed in corridors, sunrooms, anywhere there was space. The hospital became so busy that the usual classwork for the nursing students was postponed until November, and the annual "Donation Day" was not held.

The nurses worked long days and nights, and every nurse was needed. The increased number of patients meant more work, and some of the influenza patients were so ill they died. The nurses provided such good care that one report indicates that no person hospitalized for other reasons caught the flu. At times though, the nurse could do little more than go from one patient to the next giving fluids and trying to reduce fevers. In spite of the many cases of influenza necessitating long hours, very few nurses became ill, and those who did were not seriously afflicted.*

Late in 1918 the war ended. Soldiers and nurses returned home, and physicians came back to the hospital. One Mary Hitchcock graduate remained abroad to work with the Near East Commission, but none of the nurses from the school were war casualties.

In the spring and summer of 1919 fewer women applied to the nursing school for admission than in previous years. This coupled with a high attrition rate among probationers rendered the school incapable of retaining its full complement of nurses. A decrease in the number of nursing students created a serious problem as the hospital could not provide previous levels of service with fewer nurses.

Miss Shepard, in her farsighted manner, thought that the problem might be alleviated in part by adopting the eight hour day for students. It had been tried in a few places and was thought to be productive. She wrote in 1919 that she hoped the eight hour plan "... may, before long, be introduced in the New Hampshire schools of nursing." She did not

* The Alumnae Association contributed a sum of money for the cost of the service flag which was carried proudly by nursing students in Hanover's Liberty Loan parade.

* The following year, 1919, brought severe cases of influenza to the nursing school and hospital. Many students and hospital workers were stricken at once. When Miss Shepard and the head nurse were both ill, the hospital's nursing service was well managed by the students.

live to see it, however, as it was many years before her goal was implemented at Mary Hitchcock.

In 1920 the school began supplying the students with books and uniforms, thus allowing them greater financial liberty with the monthly stipend. In addition the new Billings-Lee Home offered very pleasant living quarters. These two features undoubtedly attracted students to the school, and full or near full enrollment was maintained in the following years.*

* The Committee for the Study of Nursing and Nursing Education in the United States reported in 1923 that most hospital schools did not offer an appealing introduction to nursing. Students were expected to accept long, sometimes erratic hours, unnecessary and noneducational duties, poor living conditions, and rigid discipline. The committee charged that in order to compete with other professions in attracting desirable students schools should raise their standards, correct adverse qualities, and promote a less discouraging concept of nursing.

Part 2

Growth

5

Postwar Adjustment

WORLD WAR I WAS BARELY given over to historians when the country began to feel changes in its way of life. Prewar attitudes were cast aside as Americans welcomed the products of advancing technology and economic prosperity. The automobile, radio, motion pictures, and the growth of leisure time intensified the prevailing sense of well-being. Rigid codes of etiquette had begun to relax and the "Jazz Age" was ushered in by the younger generation's new music, dances, dress, and conventions.

Prohibition, a hotly contested issue, went into effect in January 1920 and remained law until 1933. The women's rights movement not only supported and facilitated passage of the prohibition amendment but gained a momentous victory when Congress gave women the vote in 1920. Women also responded to new fashion mandates by shortening their skirts and bobbing their hair.

Medical science continued to flourish. Successes in the operating rooms and laboratories throughout the country and in Canada were encouraging. In 1921 thousands of diabetics were given new hope when the field of endocrinology opened. It had been determined that insulin was the substance in the pancreas necessary to the body's metabolic process. Pernicious anemia, once life threatening, was deemed treatable by dietary additions of liver. As diseases were studied the death rate from diphtheria, typhoid, and cholera declined while the life expectancy of Americans increased.

Public health programs had been active in large cities since the turn of the century. Now, with a growing awareness and concern for health, the movement spread to more rural areas. Concepts of health care, preventive medicine, and information about birth control were available to adults, and schools attempted to teach children good health habits.* The nurse's role was expanding as schools and community agencies became aware of the value of a public health nurse, but some questioned whether a nurse could "teach" in addition to nursing the sick.

In 1920 there were nearly three thousand training schools in the United States. Some of these schools were carefully organized and professionally administered and turned out well-educated nurses. The National League for Nursing Education had for some time given its approval of "accreditation" to those schools which met prescribed standards. However, there were many inferior schools which were not accredited but continued to graduate poorly prepared nurses.

Members of the American Nurses' Association (ANA), the National Organization of Public Health Nurses (NOPHN), and the National League for Nursing Education (NLNE), began to consider the future of nursing. Through these professional alliances the membership of these organizations endorsed the work of two comprehensive surveys which brought nursing under very close scrutiny.

The Committee for the Study of Nursing and Nursing Education in the United States, sponsored by the Rockefeller Foundation, was organized in 1919 and began its extensive look at nursing. In 1923 the famous Goldmark Report declared that nursing education primarily took place in apprentice-like situations where students were exploited as cheap labor sources and used to the hospitals' best advantage. It also cited glaring unprofessional practices found in some of the schools surveyed: lack of supervision of students, inordinate working hours, unqualified teachers, low educational standards, use of students for nonnursing duties, and use of students as head nurses. While acknowledging that progress has been made, the committee pointed out that nursing education needed fundamental changes including further development of collegiate programs to provide for the education of nursing leaders.

In 1926 the Committee on the Grading of Nurses began its eighth year of work. This group was financed partly by nurses themselves, and had representatives from the three national nursing groups in its

* The first birth control clinic in the United States was opened in New York in 1916 by a nurse, Margaret H. Sanger. She was a pioneer in this field and as a nurse activist spent her life educating the public in the controversial subject.

membership. The ambitious project encompassed three separate investigations including the actual grading of nursing schools. In 1928 the first report was issued following the study of supply and demand. "Nurses, Patients, and Pocketbooks" warned against the current oversupply of nurses, poorly trained nurses, and inferior educational conditions.

In October 1929 the stock market crashed and "The Roaring Twenties" were silenced. For nearly a decade Americans would endure the hardships of economic collapse, unemployment, and insecurity. Along with others, nurses too would face devastating circumstances as a great depression swept the country.

The Pike House was a welcome change from the crowded quarters at the hospital.

The Hospital Expands

The decade following World War I proved to be a time of professional growth and physical expansion for the Mary Hitchcock Memorial Hospital. Hints of change could be sensed and the continued support of the town of Hanover, Dartmouth College, and area towns helped the hospital maintain its high level of service as it accommodated these changes so necessary to its future.

In 1919 the trustees were confronted with a shortage of student nurses. Nationwide reports of this situation threatened grave consequences. Edwin J. Bartlett, then president of the hospital wrote,

. . . No nurses means no hospital in operation. . . . Those who seek nursing as the profession of their choice will continue to come to the hospitals for training, but may

be expected to look more carefully into the conditions under which their work is to be done . . . their conditions of life must be made comfortable, their hours of rest and recreation pleasant and their surroundings as homelike as possible.

Therefore, after much consideration and speculation the trustees determined that ". . . for the sake of the hospital's future . . ." a new nurses' home should be built. Plans were drawn up quickly and a site on the northwest corner of the hospital grounds was chosen for the new building. The entire hospital family, especially the nurses, watched the construction with interest. It was completed in July 1920.

For several years the Hanover Women's Club had raised funds for various hospital needs.* This group gradually assumed management of the hospital's annual "Donation Day" and with the cooperation of clubs in area communities the event continued to be a great success. Those connected with the hospital were aware of the importance of the gifts of fresh and canned vegetables, staple foods, linens, and money. It was not unusual for the hospital to receive several months' supplies of these items on Donation Day. Hospital workers gratefully acknowledged these yearly gifts.

As hospital services were increased continual improvements were made where feasible and equipment was added when necessary. Modernization added to the comforts inside the hospital while acquisitions of equipment such as a motor-driven lawn mover (to replace the horse-drawn one) eased the outdoor maintenance.

In September 1927 Dick Hall's House was opened to receive students and unmarried men of the Dartmouth community. It was given to the college by Mr. and Mrs. Edward K. Hall in memory of their son, Richard Drew Hall, Dartmouth Class of 1927. "Dick's House" was more than an infirmary and it provided various health services over the years to Dartmouth students and personnel. This in part relieved some of the crowding that had troubled the hospital.

Also in 1927 a three-story service addition which connected A and B wing and the operating room was built. It contained dining rooms, employee quarters, and a classroom. Outdoor parking spaces, concrete sidewalks, and a driveway were constructed. These improvements and additions, completed in 1928, had been carefully planned with the ultimate growth of Mary Hitchcock Hospital in mind.

* The Hanover Women's Club had been a devoted exponent of the hospital and was very generous to that facility and the school of nursing. Many items and monetary gifts were donated by the club and its Hospital Aid Committee endeavored to further that organization's hospital work. Members contributed large amounts of time to hospital projects and the hospital and the women enjoyed a pleasant relationship.

Professional Advances

The annual report of the trustees in 1922 carried the note of the resignation of Ida Frances Shepard, R.N. She was ". . . at her own request relieved of her duties as Superintendent . . ." in February, 1922. She remained at the hospital in another capacity however; she served as recorder in the office. Miss Shepard was replaced by Miss Harriet W. Horton, R.N. (MHMH Class of 1905) who had worked at the hospital since 1916. Miss Horton remained in the superintendent's position for a year, and in May 1923 Miss Anna C. Lockerby, R.N. assumed the duties.

In 1927 the hospital experienced a major reorganization when Miss Lockerby resigned. It was apparent that the responsibilities of the superintendent had become so diverse that a division was necessary. Therefore Miss Hazel Bryant, R.N. was appointed superintendent of nurses while James A. Hamilton took over duties as superintendent of the hospital. This division worked out well for the hospital's nursing service because many of Mr. Hamilton's duties were concerned with nonnursing matters, and the superintendent of nurses was quite occupied with the business of the nursing school and the hospital's nursing care. In 1928 Miss Rose E. Griffin, R.N. succeeded Miss Bryant and after Miss Shepard's retirement was the first superintendent of nurses to remain at the hospital for more than a few years.

The physicians on the hospital staff took a progressive stride when they formed the Hitchcock Clinic in 1927. This form of group practice enabled them to provide an even higher level of service to patients as well as to enhance their own professional growth. This full-time staff organization lent itself to teaching as well as to the practice of medicine, and in the years to come students as well as patients would benefit.

By 1929 the hospital had operated at a loss for three consecutive years. Even though the income to the facility had grown it was offset by rising costs. This was indeed an indication of things to come as Hanover and the rest of the nation entered the Great Depression.

The Training School

In slightly more than a quarter of a century the Mary Hitchcock Memorial Hospital Training School for Nurses had increased its student enrollment from two to twenty-seven in 1920. Even with the additional living quarters of the Pike House, the school was crowded beyond its limits. The construction of the new nurses' residence was therefore cause for excitement and joy among members of the school.

On July 30, 1920, a reception was held at the home and the Billings-Lee Residence was officially opened. All interested persons were invited to inspect the residence and the nurses in training moved in immediately afterward.

The three-story white wooden building was tastefully designed and contained rooms for thirty-six nurses and the superintendent. On the first floor the living room, furnished by the Women's Club of Hanover,

The Billings-Lee Residence during the winter of 1921.

provided a pleasant atmosphere in which to read, visit with friends, or relax. The basement housed a classroom and a laundry. Each nurse's room was wallpapered and painted and furnished with a white enameled bed, a good-sized rug, a bureau, table, straight chair, and a rocking chair. The nurses were so pleased with their new home that Ida Shepard exclaimed ". . . It far surpasses anything we had ever thought possible for us to possess."

Since 1901 Miss Shepard had seen the Mary Hitchcock Hospital and Training School grow into a recognized and highly respected health center. While teaching young women to be nurses, she had diligently pursued the advancement of the profession. She led the training school and hospital through times of prosperity, growth, hardship, and a world war. In February 1922 with the accomplishments of these years behind her, she asked to be relieved of the superintendent's duties. With expressed regret the trustees accepted her resignation, and Miss Shepard moved into living quarters in the hospital and continued her devoted service to the institution in the position of recorder.

Typical student room in Billings-Lee during the 1920s.

During the next six years the school was managed by three different superintendents. Each of these women brought to the position her own experience and skills while the school continued to provide nurses with a sound, well-rounded, training. Miss Horton was intimately familiar with the school, having been a head nurse at Mary Hitchcock as well as having been assistant to Miss Shepard. She capably assumed the superintendent's position in 1922. Miss Lockerby had also been a head nurse here. Miss Bryant was a former supervisor. Although each of these women served short terms, their sense of responsiblity and determination carried the school through a period of change.

Changes Ahead

The Mary Hitchcock Training School had become a well-known school and each year there were more inquiries about the program. Although this was an unsettled time for nursing, there were many women who wanted to enter the profession. Those desiring to attend the school in Hanover had a variety of reasons for choosing this career. Several had older sisters or relatives who were nurses, some had "always wanted to be a nurse," some were influenced by physicians, and others simply thought it was a good idea.

At the beginning of the decade nursing pupils were still admitted singly as vacancies occurred. In 1922 it was decided to increase the enrollment from twenty-seven to twenty-nine students in order to have two nurses available for special duty when patients required such care. Miss Horton noted that this not only provided extra comfort to the patients but ". . . a source of income for the hospital."

The New Hampshire State Board of Education recommended in 1923 that the Mary Hitchcock Training School admit students in classes rather than one at a time. In September 1924 a class of twelve women entered the school, followed by six in January 1925. This method of admissions to the program was more satisfactory than the old way and was adopted as policy.

Private duty nursing was still the domain of most graduates of Mary Hitchcock. The private duty nurse went into the homes of patients, traveled with them, or remained at the hospital to care for them. (In 1922 there was a total of forty-nine graduate private duty nurses used on special cases at Mary Hitchcock.) Private duty was still twenty or twenty-four hours a day and the nurses in the hospital still slept on a cot in the patient's room. During the next decade however, the private duty nurses began to work twelve hour days.

Although most nurses preferred the private cases, other areas of nursing were becoming available to graduates. Industrial nursing, public health and some hospital positions were starting to attract nurses. Many Mary Hitchcock women took postgraduate courses (usually in larger city hospitals) and explored these new areas. By 1923 Grafton County as well as the Town of Hanover employed public health nurses and several Hitchcock nurses with postgraduate work in public health returned to the Upper Valley to provide citizens with health care and education.

The school had always attempted to follow the guidelines set by the National League for Nursing Education and reported yearly to the

Probationary students learning practical nursing skills in Billings-Lee classroom, 1928.

New Hampshire State Board of Nursing. In 1927 the school revised its curriculum in conjunction with the League's guide. That same year the use of the title "Instructor" first appeared in school records. Miss Ellen Boyle, R.N. is listed as the first nurse associated with the school to be designated instructor, although her predecessors in student work performed the same duties.

A course in mental diseases was added in 1928-1929. For several years Professor Chauncy C. Allen of Dartmouth College instructed the students in the theoretical aspects of emotional illness while Miss Griffin taught the nursing component. There was no practical experience in the care of the emotionally ill at this time, but the nurses traveled to Brattleboro, Vermont, to the Brattleboro Retreat for a one day observational experience. In 1929 it was a sizable undertaking to transport fourteen students seventy five miles and back.

The school grew quickly and the once spacious Billings-Lee home gradually became crowded. By 1928 there were thirty-five students and Miss Bryant declared that additional rooms for the women and classroom space and library were absolutely necessary. The following year the Billings-Lee basement classroom was converted into a refer-

Reference library in the basement of Billings-Lee, 1928.

ence library, and a large new classroom was added. Meanwhile the school continued to grow and the students continued to crowd into the living quarters.

The Alumnae Association continued its regular meetings which were well-attended. Annual reunions were popular and met with success as alumnae returned to the school each year to see old friends, learn of each others' nursing endeavors, and observe changes within the school.

As the twenties neared their end a new superintendent of nurses, Miss Rose E. Griffin, R.N., joined the school where she remained for twelve years. Miss Griffin was energetic and led the school into a new era of nursing. In the annual report of 1928-1929 the word "training" had been deleted and the school was referred to as the Mary Hitchcock Memorial Hospital School of Nursing. That same year the first school prospectus, or catalogue, was published and the first full-time instructor in diet therapy was hired. It was also recorded that the school was among those first to participate in the voluntary grading by the Committee on the Grading of Nursing Schools in 1929.

The school had also grown in its administration. In 1929 the census of the school listed seven nurses and others responsible for the instruction of its students. The 1920s had been a time of change and served to bridge the transition from old to new. The school, now past its infancy, was ready to embrace the future of nursing.*

For many the school's link with the past was severed in May 1929 with the death of Ida Frances Shepard. A friend and devoted servant of the school and hospital was gone. She had loved "Mary's House" and had dedicated nearly all her professional life and work to it. In the words of Miss Griffin, "... for twenty-eight years she reflected honor and glory on this hospital and school."

Five months later the Crash of '29 set in motion unforseen changes which Hanover and the Mary Hitchcock Memorial Hospital School of Nursing would face along with the rest of the world.

* In 1928 the Edward C. Daniels Fund was established for the recreation and entertainment of the student nurses of the school. (This fund later provided for annual scholarships for postgraduate study by a graduating nurse.) Other major gifts to the nursing school were the Lillian Louise Knox Fund, established in 1961 as a loan fund for students, and the Ernest N. Seavey Fund for the school library. The Alumnae Association also contributed to the school with various gifts over the years.

6

Student Life

STUDENT NURSES of this time lived very differently than other young people since they spent most of their time in the rather sequestered environment of Mary Hitchcock. They received instruction and assumed the roles of nurses while their lifestyles were centered around the hospital and school. At an early age they were committed to an exacting profession which required maturity, diligence, and long hours of work and study.

After the Billings-Lee Nurses Home opened only the new probationers lived in the hospital and then for only a short period. Usually when probation was completed they moved over to Billings-Lee. Upon arrival at the school the new students were usually greeted by the superintendent, or her representative, and shown to the third floor of the hospital where as many as eight girls might share a room. The third floor was also occupied by the hospital maids and earned the nickname of "French Flat." Some accounts also indicate that possibly the nurses slept in the small attic space on top of the third floor quarters, climbing up a ladder-like set of stairs to their beds. This too had nicknames (not mentioned) since the space was small, crowded, and noisy due to the nearby water tower which dripped constantly making sleep difficult.

Life on the third floor had its disadvantages. One of the more distressing aspects of living there was the fact that the stairway was open from the rotunda of the hospital, on the first floor, all the way up to the third floor. On the second floor were the private rooms, directly beneath the probationers' quarters. Sometimes, especially in the evening, the nurses' youthful exuberance bubbled over and the noise of laughter and conversation carried throughout the hospital. On these occasions the night supervisor would notify the offending persons to dress in uniform and come down to the rotunda. The students would then have to spend the evening sitting there, supposedly studying, until permission was received to return upstairs. This was not a desirable way to spend an evening, and eventually the seats where the students sat in the rotunda, near the fireplace, became known as the "anxious seats."

The early days of a probationer's schooling were primarily devoted to learning the proper way to clean utility rooms, make beds, scrub the copper hoppers, polish silver, and dust floors. Care of the patient's flowers was also emphasized. Gradually the nurses were taught general patient care (bathing, feeding, turning, and backrubs), basic nursing procedures, and the reasons for doing them. After completing the probationary time a student received her cap and usually went on night duty.

The students of the 1920s did not have a much easier schedule than their earlier counterparts. They were still expected to put in long days (7:00 A.M. to 7:00 P.M. with a two hour break) and had a half day off each week. Often classes were held on their free time. An addition to the daily schedule during this time was the institution of daily chapel services, held each morning in Billings-Lee. Attendance was mandatory for day nurses and attendance was taken. The short devotions were held before breakfast and at times an impromptu inspection was held. Uniform, shoes, and stockings had to be neat, clean, and worn in the prescribed manner.

Following chapel students went to breakfast in the hospital dining room. Every attempt was made to be on time, for lateness resulted in some penalty, usually the loss of an evening "late permission" and these were precious. After breakfast the nurses arrived on the wards before 7:00 A.M. for the day's work. There were baths to give, vital signs to observe, trays to pass, patients to feed, treatments to administer, and cleaning to be done or delegated to someone else.

On an extremely busy ward a student might find herself with eight or more patients to care for in addition to other duties. She was not excused for class or her two hour break until all her duties were completed. If work was not finished by the time of the assigned break the nurse finished it as quickly as possible, for the free time would not be changed. If a ward was busier than usual the charge nurse or the

The hospital's elegant architecture enhanced the transmission of sound, and the third floor students tried to maintain a quiet atmosphere.

Students assembled for meals in the hospital dining room.

hospital's head nurse might decide that the students could not attend class that day since they were needed in the hospital. Some of the cooking was still done on the wards, and the nurse often found herself cooking eggs and making toast as part of the day's routine.

A certain system of rank, almost military in nature, had evolved by now. The third year or senior nurses were the locus of power within the nursing hierarchy. With only the superintendent, her assistant, and one head nurse, these seniors were used as charge nurses.* They were given almost total responsibility for the administration and nursing care on their ward, and took their assignments very seriously. All the younger nurses were under their bidding, and usually in awe of the senior nurse. At meals in the dining room the nurses sat at one table and the house staff at another. When gathered for a meal the nurses could not take their seats until a senior nurse arrived at the table, and then her permission had to be obtained in order to be excused. This rank system extended downward to the newest pro-

* The hospital did from time to time hire a graduate nurse to help oversee the wards and supervise students. There is a record of one such graduate nurse being at the hospital in 1924.

bationer for no nurse ever walked in front of a nurse who was senior to her in training. In addition only senior nurses could sit down while on duty. Young nurses respected and perhaps feared the senior nurses and looked forward to the day when they would assume that coveted role.

The hospital had become affectionately known to the students as "Mary's House." All who entered became aware of the aura of warmth, yet of professionalism in the staff. There was a certain closeness among the members of the school and hospital staff, and kindness, sincerity, and respect were expected from and awarded to each person there.

Many classroom hours were spent learning the basic theories of nursing.

The student nurses were ambassadors of goodwill in addition to being hospital workers. Many patients came to associate the warmth and good care of Mary's House with the student nurses whom they encountered.

Christmas was a special time at Mary Hitchcock. The old tradition of giving Christmas presents to patients was still maintained, and the hospital was festooned with decorations for the season. For some students it was also a difficult time. Many a homesick young nurse, spending her first Christmas away from home and family, shed tears as she wrapped garlands of greenery around the bannister of the great staircase that stretched upward from the rotunda. In celebration of the holiday the nurses often gave a Christmas party or a play, and invited their friends. The effort was made to have as cheerful a holiday as possible.

The training school still had to provide the hospital with its night nurses. A night supervisor was employed to assist the students and oversee the hospital, but the night nurse was largely on her own in charge of the assigned ward. If someone was very ill or recovering from anesthesia, the nurse spent most of her night caring for that patient. If two patients needed her at once she could try to reach the supervisor for help, or more often decide the priority herself and do the best she could. The night usually passed quickly with vital signs to monitor, medications to give (there was only one narcotic cupboard for the hospital), and charts to write. The nurse sat at a small desk in the hall outside the wards. The next day she could sleep, but if a class was scheduled she had to attend. Night duty lasted from one to three months, seven nights a week, 7:00 P.M. to 7:00 A.M. At the end of the assigned rotation the student nurse received two days off and could go home if she obtained permission from the superintendent.

The bulk of the nurse's practical training in nursing was received by working on the general medical and surgical wards, caring for patients with a wide variety of illnesses. Here theories could be integrated while the student observed a broad range of medical and surgical disorders. Lectures on these disorders were given by physicians while the nursing care was taught by the nurses. Students were rotated from ward to ward or service to service about every three months. When a student was going to a general medical or surgical ward, she was sometimes asked which ward she preferred. It had been determined that the nurses worked better and with more satisfaction on a ward which they liked.

In addition to the general services, students had some practical experience on a variety of special services. These were always looked forward to with delight, as in the case of pediatrics or obstetrics, or with dread as in the case of diet kitchen. Some students liked the operating room experience, others hated it.

The obstetrical rotation was usually one of the more popular. Here the students helped with deliveries, then cared for the babies and mothers. At this time the babies were kept in a nursery separate from the mothers. It was mostly a pleasant working experience and the students enjoyed it.

The pediatric experience was also well liked by students as children were of interest to most of the young women. The number of children cared for in the hospital was, however, of concern to the State Board of Education. The small number of pediatric cases was considered insufficient to constitute a broad enough clinical experience, and in 1924 some thought was given to the possibility of setting up an affiliated experience in pediatric nursing at an institution that cared for more children.

The time spent in the diet kitchen was calculated to acquaint the student with the theories of nutritional therapeutics and also to teach basic elements of nutrition for everyday living. In practice, the students cooked the special diet foods, baked salt-free bread, and to their horror, ground up raw liver and mixed it with orange juice for the anemic patients.

The operating room, or O.R. rotation, was one that required the students to perform a variety of tasks. They set up the room for operations, assisted with surgeries, and cleaned the room after the case was finished. The experience lasted three months and the students would occasionally be on call at night. If an emergency surgery came up the nurse on call would be awakened by the night supervisor to go to the operating room to prepare, assist, and clean up. It there was time she went back to bed to catch some sleep before the next day's cases. If not, she worked right through. Students were also taught to give ether, and many administered it for operations.

As in earlier years nursing students had little free time to engage in social or recreational activities, but they were resourceful in using the time they had. Rules were still very strict and the girls were carefully supervised. Young women were expected to behave as ladies, and little compassion was given for the inexperience and abandon of youth.

Automobiles were becoming more common around Hanover and the nurses were warned against "joy riders" and were forbidden to hitchhike. Fraternity houses were off limits, except for special permission, and a close record was kept of where students went and when (and often with whom). A student might easily find herself being told that her nursing was suffering due to her excessive social life.

Late permissions were available, but infractions of other rules resulted in the loss of these. Regularly, students had to be in by ten, a late permission could let one stay out until eleven or twelve o'clock. In either case a student returning to the nurses' home in the evening had to enter the hospital and sign in near the office. If she should be late someone was sure to notice and she would be reported. Therefore it can be assumed that more than one student nurse has been helped in through the boiler room by some kindly hospital engineer.

Part of the student body in 1928. Although hemlines were raised, waists dropped, and high laced shoes had disappeared, the uniform remained basically unchanged.

Nurses frequently held parties and dances at the home. Friends were invited to these activities and for a time it was customary to exchange dancing parties with the students of the medical school.

Cultural and educational opportunities were made available by Dartmouth College, and many of the young women took the opportunity to enjoy these. In addition the college recreational facilities were accessible and nurses played tennis, skated, skied, went sledding, and walked through the campus, sometimes in the company of the young men of the college.

7

The Depression Years

IN 1931 former President Calvin Coolidge wrote in his syndicated newspaper column, "The country is not in good condition." The stock market crash in October 1929 had signaled a downward spiral of the American economy as production, employment, and foreign trade fell. This overwhelming trend persisted and in 1932 nearly 25 percent of American workers were without jobs. Meanwhile banks closed, businesses failed, and Americans were forced to line up for food handouts as mass unemployment consumed the labor force.

There were widespread reports of financial ruin, personal loss, and suicide as many citizens encountered poverty and despair. In large cities soup kitchens and breadlines were commonplace, and camps or shantytowns known as "Hoovervilles" sprang up. Sometimes these makeshift settlements were located near town dumps where their hapless inhabitants combed the trash heaps to retrieve the rubbish discarded by the more fortunate.

For nearly ten years federal, state, and local governments wrestled with the problems burdening a depressed nation. The administration shouldered the task of rebuilding the economy while providing temporary relief for desperate citizens. Several newly created agencies offered aid to the indigent as well as to institutions, and provided some jobs. Still, millions of Americans suffered abject poverty.

Despite the hardships imposed by the Depression, scientific research continued and the first "wonder drugs," the sulfonamides, were discovered. Medical technology was developed and modern devices to promote the comfort and safety of patients were marketed. Other machines helped lighten work loads as they added efficiency to patient care. Hospital personnel were able to ensure a higher level of care as they found their work easier.

Few individuals could afford the services of a private nurse and were cared for by the "floor duty" nurses when they entered the hospital. Most hospitals relied on their nursing students for hospital work and as a result thousands of graduate nurses joined the ranks of the unemployed. In some areas private duty nurses began to divide the day into three eight hour "shifts" to spread the available work.*

The *American Journal of Nursing* published letters and statements from nursing groups around the country announcing that there was little or no work for nurses, thus advising others not to relocate in hope of finding jobs. In 1932 and 1933 many hospital administrators debated whether to hire graduate nurses for floor duty in exchange for their room and board. These grave developments led the American Nurses Association to endorse a plan calling for the eight-hour working day, and the gradual termination of some training schools. Little or no job security had given the future a bleak outlook, and remembering old warnings against overproduction nursing leaders and hospital administrators viewed a troubled profession.

As the effects of the Depression worsened, the government implemented programs to boost the economy and provide work for many of the unemployed. Positions for nurses were offered by the Federal Emergency Relief Fund, the Civil Works Administration, and the Works Progress Administration. Most of these jobs were public health related and involved needy families. The Civil Works Administration alone hired more than ten thousand nurses. After the Social Security Act had been passed many nurses received stipends for public health training and went back to school.*

Nursing educators were forced to look carefully at nursing education and in 1937 the National League for Nursing Education revised its curriculum guide for diploma schools, presenting new premises of nursing education. First, the NLNE stated that the primary function of

* Although work was very scarce for graduates, the field of air travel opened with new roles for nurses. A basic requirement for air hostesses was that they be registered nurses and many women took on this new and exciting work.

* Many nurses had gone on relief, some of whom were unable to accept government jobs until they had been given clothing and shoes.

nursing schools was to educate nurses, and secondly, to recognize nurses' responsibility to the community as well as to the hospital.

With these new concepts as a base, the curriculum guide proposed reasonable work hours for students with regularly scheduled classes. Periods for study, recreation, and rest were considered mandatory, and a preclinical term with no hospital work and preparatory classes was suggested. New emphasis was placed on the psychological and social aspects of health and illness. Programs of study and practice were encouraged to promote integration of theory and nursing care.

The nursing profession emerged from the Depression with a stronger educational framework for its schools. During that time many diploma schools were closed, and by 1936 there were about seventy collegiate programs. In addition, hospitals began to hire graduates and more positions opened for registered nurses. Just as nursing settled down to its new endeavors, boiling international affairs threatened a war which would change the world.

The Hospital

The Mary Hitchcock Memorial Hospital faced the challenges of the Depression with the loyal support of the town of Hanover, Dartmouth College, and area towns. The facility needed repairs, renovations, equipment, and expansion, and these needs were met during a time of economic hardship.

The Carter X-ray Building opened in 1930 and the Eye Clinic was established in 1932. By 1938 the hospital had added a new heating plant, laundry, and nurses' residence, each complete with new equipment for operation. In addition there was a four-story wing next to the Carter building which housed laboratories, a surgical suite, obstetrical and pediatric units, and the hospital's first elevator. With a few corridor modifications it served the entire facility. A new building housed the Hitchcock Clinic and small additions were made to the old East and West wards. These tiny areas added to the physical space of the wards but personnel referred to them as "the cracker boxes." The hospital then had a bed capacity of one hundred and sixty-four and Dick Hall's House thirty-two.

A very significant development of that time was the founding of the Mary Hitchcock Memorial Hospital Auxiliary. This well-organized group assumed various fund-raising activities for the hospital and purchased materials and equipment. It also presented gifts to the nursing school over the years and volunteers gave countless hours of service to patients in the hospital.*

As the Depression continued the bed occupancy of the hospital declined while more patient accounts went unpaid. Strict economy was necessary in the purchase of all supplies and fuel. The State Relief of New Hampshire was able to give the hospital assistance in its payment of some accounts and the free or endowed bed system was revised to provide more revenue for the hospital. Throughout the Depression Mary Hitchcock continued to provide service with no decrease in quality. Generous citizens and a dedicated staff did their share to maintain the high standards.

Personnel

In 1931 the hospital set up a registry for graduate nurses who were doing private duty. This was thought to be of benefit to the community as well as individual nurses. In 1932-1933 the members of the registry agreed to reduce their fee to $5.00 for twelve hours of nursing in hope of obtaining more work. However, the demand for private nurses fell, and the following year each nurse averaged only 191 days of work. This was scarcely enough to live on and during the difficult winter of 1934 the hospital stood ready to accept registry nurses for hospital duty in order that they have food and shelter. Fortunately this did not prove necessary, and by 1936 there was a noticeable improvement in employment for the private duty nurses.

As the hospital grew and enlarged its services the administration of the facility became more complex. More personnel were required to insure efficient operation. While each department added employees, the hospital endeavored to hire more graduates, and in 1935 each patient care unit had a graduate nurse to direct nursing care and supervise students. In 1936 Superintendent James A. Hamilton resigned and was succeeded by Donald S. Smith

The Depression presented many problems, but these were met and solved as Mary Hitchcock continued to develop as a health center. Continued goodwill and pleasant relations with citizens of the Upper Valley prevailed. Many of these citizens would fill yet another need when a major war disrupted the world.

* The Auxiliary, established in 1933 has continued to provide unexcelled volunteer and fund-raising service to the hospital. Its members were the forerunners of today's social service in their aid to distressed families. Today the group maintains the gift shop in the hospital and assists in many hospital services.

The Nursing School

The transitional period of the previous decade led Mary Hitchcock nursing school personnel to the questions and challenges posed by the 1930s. As Miss Griffin directed the school through the rigors of the Depression, she also devoted much thought and energy to solving the new problems of nursing and nursing education at Mary Hitchcock.

In 1930 the school received the report from the first Committee on the Grading of Nursing Schools. In an effort to enable schools to evaluate and upgrade their programs the committee focused on areas for improvement. School officials at Mary Hitchcock were well aware of the program's shortcomings and thus were not surprised at the contents of the committee report. Among the concerns raised were: lack of student supervision (beyond the preliminary period), limited student understanding of medical and surgical nursing, lack of opportunities for student rest and recreation, excessive work hours for students, fatigue among the student body, and the lack of funding or endowment for the school.

Miss Griffin and her assistants were hopeful that the school could accommodate the recommendations of the grading committee as well as meet the current standards for nursing schools as prescribed by the National League for Nursing Education. Both groups recommended an eight-hour day for students, including hospital work and classes! In addition, the requirements for theoretical instruction were increasing, meaning additional classroom hours. Although Miss Griffin thoroughly understood the difficulties presented at this time she and the other educators worked hard to accomplish this sizeable task. Not only were these women accountable to the nursing students for their education, but they were also responsible for the efficient delivery of nursing service throughout the hospital.

Keeping abreast of innovations and changing standards within the nursing profession required dedication and energy. The New Hampshire Board of Nurse Examiners, or simply the "State Board," attempted to follow the NLNE guidelines as much as possible and governed the state's schools in their adoption of certain criteria. As the accepted curriculum was revised and expanded more courses were necessary to provide the increased content. The school at Mary Hitchcock began to adopt new courses in its curriculum, but the teaching faculty did not increase proportionately. Instead, the nurses assumed more classroom teaching in addition to hospital duties.

In 1930 there was one designated instructor at the school to teach basic nursing arts and theory. This was her sole responsibility. Other nursing courses were taught by the nurse supervisors or Miss Griffin. Each supervisor of a specialty area taught the content for that subject, such as obstetrics, operating room technique, and so on. A dietician was responsible for instructing the students in dietetics while physicians and others lectured on selected topics.

In 1932 the school participated in the second grading of nursing schools and the following year the report from this committee was received. One of the charges to the school administrators asked that they seriously examine the feasibility of maintaining an undergraduate school as opposed to employing a larger graduate nurse staff. In his annual report of 1933 James Hamilton revealed the administration's decision to keep the school open.

In accordance with the general recommendations of the Second Grading of the Committee on the Grading of Nursing Schools, we have considered carefully whether we should maintain an undergraduate school of nursing or supplant it in part or whole by a graduate staff. We have concluded that there is place in the system of nursing education for an undergraduate school at our hospital and that we have adequate personnel and faculties for such operation . . . we do feel as a contribution to the unemployment situation of graduate nurses that we should temporarily reduce the number of our pupils . . . our study emphasized the advisability of employing more graduate nurses . . . we hope funds will permit these long delayed additions . . . Unfortunately the housing facilities for nurses are barely sufficient for our present organization.

CENSUS OF STUDENTS IN THE NURSING SCHOOL
(Annual Reports, June 30, 1932-1936)

STUDENTS:	1932-33	1933-34	1934-35	1935-36
Seniors	17	17	10	16
Intermediates	17	17	15	21
Juniors	11	8	21	13
	45	42	46	50

Note: Preliminary students had completed the specified term by June 30, and would then be listed as Juniors.

As the Depression continued many young women faced limited career options. Some who could not afford college turned to nursing and each year more women inquired about the nursing program at

Mary Hitchcock. Applications to the school increased and school personnel were careful to select students who seemed best suited for nursing. In 1933 the school began to administer the Moss and Hunt Aptitude Test for Nursing to prospective pupils, and Professor Chauncy N. Allen of Dartmouth College was helpful in the administration and interpretation of these tests. Applicants for the program were expected to be in the upper half of their high school class, to have a rich science background, and to possess intelligence, a degree of maturity, good health, and a "satisfactory" social background.

With the school having grown at a fast rate, the quarters at Billings-Lee were indeed crowded. The young women, however, accepted the fact that there was a Depression and many were simply thankful to be in school. In 1935 the Mary Hitchcock Memorial Hospital Auxiliary completely redecorated the living room of the nurses' home. While this did not alleviate the crowding, it did much to brighten the home, and the nurses were appreciative.

In 1936 construction began on the addition to Billings-Lee and in October 1937 the "37 Building" opened with a public reception. The comfortable and modern residence had forty-eight bedrooms, nine sitting rooms, bathrooms, a kitchen, a recreation room, a smoking room, and a men's lounge. In addition a roof recreation area was installed so the nurses could enjoy more sunshine during their off-duty hours. The students and school officers were pleased with their new building, but it was inadequate almost immediately and soon the familiar crowding occurred.

Student illness, in varying degrees, had been a problem at the school for some time. Indeed, it was not unusual for several students to require hospitalized treatment each year. During the early years of the school, nurses were exposed to and susceptible to many contagious diseases such as typhoid, scarlet fever, and tuberculosis. As medical science learned how to control these diseases, the incidence of such illnesses in nursing students decreased.

Around 1930 a health program for nursing students was instituted. Yearly chest X-rays were taken of each nurse. In 1931 annual physical examinations, monthly weight charts, and immunizations against typhoid, scarlet fever, and diphtheria were added. These screening aids and immunizations seemed to offer assistance in the prevention and detection of illness in the ensuing years. In 1937 it was noted that most illness occurred among second-year students who carried heavy class schedules in addition to twelve-hour night duty.

The pediatric nursing experience, long felt to be a problem at the school due to the small number of cases, gave the educators much to worry about. The state board was emphatic that the clinical experience in the nursing of children was inadequate, but during the Depression there was little that could be done about it. It was hoped that the new pediatric unit, opened in 1938, would help to correct this situation. Another concern was the lack of opportunity to care for patients with communicable diseases. Mary Hitchcock graduates doing private duty sometimes refused to take certain cases saying they felt unprepared.

The Superintendent plays host in 1932 at Billings-Lee to high school students interested in nursing careers.

As the school expanded personnel were added, and in 1938 a second instructor was hired. In 1939 the school census listed eleven nurses who taught courses and were accountable for nursing service in the hospital. There were also four ward head nurses.

During this decade nursing service and nursing education were not viewed separately at Mary Hitchcock. The inherent problems of such an arrangement made it difficult to stay on top of trends in education while providing good nursing care to hospitalized patients. One very frustrating task was that of making hospital work assignments. The person(s) responsible had to assure adequate nursing service coverage for each department twenty-four hours a day, seven days a week. Once that was assured, there were illness and leaves, each student's educational requirements, and the need to correlate theory to practice to be considered while maintaining some semblance of seniority.

Although many schools had adopted the eight-hour day for students by 1933 that was not possible at Mary Hitchcock. The school was also more than 100 hours short of the 885-hour minimum classroom teaching requirement. Miss Griffin questioned how long the school could maintain its upper rank.

As the State Board revised its curriculum requirements in accordance with the NLNE, Mary Hitchcock educators made every attempt to comply. In 1935 the school met most of the curriculum standards with the exception of a psychology course and the number of hours of theory. By now the school was 160 hours short of the recommended minimum. Miss Griffin, in the dual offices of Superintendent of Nurses, and Principal of the School of Nursing, noted " . . . Since the real objective of a nursing school is the education of the students to care for the sick, our difficulty appears to be too much education . . . " Mr. Hamilton, Superintendent of the Hospital, elaborated:

Evidently in an attempt to improve nursing education and to conform more nearly with requirements of neighboring states, the State Board of Education altered recently the curriculum requirements for schools of nursing, mainly by increasing the number of classroom hours. With a few minor exceptions these changes did not alter the curriculum structure which we have been using for the past few years. In the number of class hours, however, we are still considerably below the minimum standards established by the National League of Nursing Education many years ago and now being reviewed with the probable result of a further increase in the number of hours. One wonders, if more emphasis upon a review of the objectives of nursing education and upon the methods of instruction from an intensive viewpoint might not prove more fruitful in the development of nurses adequately trained for their places in their communities, than the extension of the subject matter to be mastered. Oftentimes deflation is more effective than inflation.

The debate was not settled at once and in 1937 Miss Griffin indicated her intention to adopt the latest revision of the NLNE Curriculum Guide. The school continued to make changes and when possible the newer trends were followed. Conscious effort by the faculty and students made the Mary Hitchcock school a leader in the state of New Hampshire. The school was always represented at the various meetings of nurses in the state, and many of the graduates were active in state nursing groups as well as their own alumnae organization. Miss

Griffin was involved in nursing affairs outside Mary Hitchcock Hospital serving as president of the New Hampshire League for Nursing and attending national conferences and meetings.

Rose Griffin felt strongly that student nurses needed a more normal life than one of such limited freedom. She stated her wish for the school to conform with newer trends, and to provide students with more leisure time including an occasional entire day free from hospital work.

A major step toward achieving this was taken in 1938 when students began an eight-hour shift of night duty on three wards (A Ward, East, and West Wards). The plan was to increase this eight-hour plan to include the entire hospital. Students were enthusiastic and hoped it would soon go into effect for all of Mary Hitchcock's wards.

At times it seemed the hospital was too large with too many services to be adequately supplied with nurses. In addition to the patient care units, the operating room, and the diet kitchen, the student nurses worked in the X-ray department, the pharmacy, and the laboratory. At times it was necessary to move students around if one area became extremely busy. (When more surgeries were performed, extra students were placed in the operating room.) When necessary, the students as well as the graduates worked extra hours. Before the new patient units opened in 1938 it had been a concern whether there were enough nurses to staff them.

By 1939 the hospital employed fourteen graduate nurses (this included the superintendent of nurses, the instructors, and the day and night supervisors, and head nurses) while the student body numbered seventy. Although short of the desirable number of nurses for the bed capacity of the hospital, these figures were better than in previous times. Again Miss Griffin urged hiring more graduates and expanding the nursing school.

The thirties had been a time of question and change at Mary Hitchcock. There were still needs, such as a better balanced clinical program for the students, but the school had survived a difficult period and emerged with a stronger education base. When war came, the Mary Hitchcock Memorial Hospital School of Nursing was prepared to do its part.

8

The Students

AS IN PAST YEARS, young women came to the Mary Hitchcock school with many reasons for wanting to become nurses. For many a lifelong dream, the advice of elders, or simply a whim had prompted application to the school, but now the Depression had made the decision for some since financial adversities limited educational opportunities.

A student's first day was taken up with arriving at the school, registering, meeting classmates, and settling into the third floor quarters of the hospital. After a tour of the complex and dinner, the evening was often spent setting up the unfamiliar uniform (stiff collar and cuffs, with black shoes and stockings), while listening to strange and often frightening hospital tales told by the upperclassmen. Lights went out by 10:00 P.M., and the new student nurse either fell asleep from exhaustion or lay awake with apprehension.

For the first month preliminary students had classes scheduled several hours each day. There they learned the theories basic to nursing and the practical skills. Under the watchful eye of the instructor or her assistant they tried out their new abilities before going to the wards to make beds, give baths, stack linen, or clean. In the evenings they studied for examinations and memorized procedures.*

* Each class of preliminary students was benefitted by the guidance of a senior nurse who assisted the instructor and helped teach and supervise. This "Senior Sister" spent her last six months in the school working with the probationary students and the instructors. School officials chose the nurse for this position.

Preliminary students were carefully monitored on the wards and did not give treatments or medications until they had been supervised and "passed" on each procedure. After the successful completion of theoretical and practical requirements, the students received their caps and became junior nurses.

At 6:00 A.M. the rising bell sounded and students arose to prepare for the day. Chapel was held in the Billings-Lee living room and attendance was mandatory. Absentees were noted and punished. On most mornings a supervisor or senior nurse directed the short prayer and hymn. Miss Griffin usually appeared only on holidays or when some "incident" had occurred. On these latter mornings fear struck the hearts of possible offenders as they awaited reprimand or worse. Reportedly, the entire student body suffered the loss of privileges when no one would confess to the "crime."

After arriving on the hospital unit and hearing the night report, students began to bathe patients, pass trays, feed patients, and make beds. One nurse on each ward gave medications while another did treatments. Each nurse received two hours off per day, and sometimes a class meant more time off the wards. If her work was unsatisfactory to her supervisors a nurse might lose her free time that day. Aside from nursing care there was plenty to do. Although the hospital had increased its maid service some cleaning was still done by the nurses. When caring for a patient in a private room the nurse was responsible for the cleanliness of that room. The nurses also washed bedpans, urinals, and emesis basins; emptied wastebaskets; and cleaned utility rooms (the hopper always needed polishing).

The day passed bringing a variety of tasks ranging from giving shaves and haircuts to arranging flowers and bedside tables. Sometimes the day's work was not finished by 7:00 P.M., and the young women pitched in to lend a hand where it was needed. Most often no one went off duty until everyone was finished.

Night assignments had not changed much and each student was required to do her share of the night work. The new junior students often found the adjustment very difficult since they still had several hours of daytime classes after working the long twelve-hour night. In addition it was sometimes hard to sleep when the day nurses spent their free time in the residence.

After the 7:00 P.M. report the student was alone on the unit until the next morning except for the occasional visit by the night supervisor or a doctor making late rounds. The night nurse was responsible for fixing the evening meal for the private duty nurse(s) on her floor and the student on private ward had to fix the tray for the night supervisor.

After patients were settled for the night there were charts to do, medications to give, and the usual night routine to follow. At each ward desk there would be a basket of materials which the night nurse was supposed to make into dressings, swabs, and operating room supplies. Ostensibly, this was to be done during the nurse's spare time, and she was expected to have completed it by morning.

Some students found that they gained valuable experience by being alone at night. Although the supervisor was available for assistance

Construction of the addition to the nursing school was well along in May, 1937.

there were times when she was not at hand and a decision had to be made immediately. (It was not unheard of for a nurse to awaken an ambulatory patient and ask him to go to the telephone and call the supervisor while she stayed with a critically ill patient.) Such experiences gradually instilled confidence in the nurse's own ability to make nursing judgments.

Each night one student was assigned to the operating room and her tasks included cleaning and preparing supplies and instruments for the following day. She scrubbed for any emergency surgeries during the night while the student on call (a daytime nurse) circulated. The operating room nurse was also liable to be called to other units to assist the night nurses when they were busy.

When the students were not on duty "home" was the living quarters of Billings-Lee, the hospital, or later the '37 Building. Here the girls made lifelong friends as they shared their secret joys and woes. Classmates grew especially close to one another, and offered friendship and support throughout the three years.

Although the superintendent of nurses and some of the supervisors and instructors lived in the residence, and some amount of order was maintained, girlish pranks and practical jokes occurred. What may have seemed juvenile and foolish to some was done good naturedly. The nurses enjoyed this fun, and rarely did it warrant the intervention of a superior.

Rules and regulations of the school were explicit and were enforced. Students were simply expected to obey the rules and for the most part they did. There were clear guidelines as to where one might go and when, and there were areas definitely off limits. Fraternities were considered off limits except for certain parties which were supervised and sanctioned by nursing school personnel. A student had to sign out when leaving hospital grounds, indicating her destination and expected time of return, and she had to sign in upon return. Late returnees were always noted and some disciplinary measure taken. Infractions of the school rules could result in expulsion from the school, suspension for a certain period of time, loss of late privileges, or being confined to the hospital grounds for a specified time.

The student nurses lived with the long hours and the restrictions on their social life, but they still had occasions for recreation and entertainment. Each year the school held organized activities for the students and their guests. Dances were favorites and the Dartmouth medical students as well as students from the college regularly joined the fun. Each spring outings were planned, the students and guests attending sugaring-off parties and other affairs. The supervisors or occasionally one of the older student nurses chaperoned these events.

After the '37 Building opened the recreation room allowed more indoor activities such as Ping-Pong. The sun deck on the roof of the new residence proved a popular area, and the pastime of sunbathing there has continued to the present time.

Free time was also spent horseback riding, skating on Occum Pond, hiking, or playing tennis. The girls were also fond of shopping in Lebanon or other nearby towns, but transportation was sometimes a problem. The school strictly enforced the rule prohibiting hitchhiking by student nurses. An account of this time tells of a small group of students who were hitchhiking back to Hanover from Lebanon after such a shopping trip. A car stopped for them and as they approached it they recognized the driver as one of the staff physicians from Mary Hitchcock. As they got into the car each felt that this meant certain expulsion from school. Back in Hanover they waited anxiously for the summons from Miss Griffin. Days passed and it did not come. Only then did they realize that the doctor had not told a soul of their exploit.

During the years of the Depression students at Mary Hitchcock adjusted to the necessary changes as they maintained their high nursing standards. They continued to work long hours while they accepted the strict discipline basic to that program. Orders were taken as such, and rarely questioned unless a patient's welfare was in jeopardy. These young women who gave so much to nursing were imaginative and fun-loving. They found pleasure in companionship as they worked, studied, and played together. As the Depression waned, the nurses at Mary Hitchcock looked forward to the new decade, unaware of the greater task which lay ahead.

9

Nursing In World War II

IN 1937 an undeclared war erupted between China and Japan, and in 1938 Hitler invaded Austria. One by one countries became involved as the conflict spread throughout Europe and the South Pacific. The United States took a neutral pose, although in March 1941 the Lend-Lease Act authorized the supplying of American war materials to allies fighting against the Axis powers. On December 7, 1941, the Japanese bombed the naval operation at Pearl Harbor, Hawaii, seriously damaging the U.S. Pacific Fleet. On December 8 the Congress of the United States declared war on Japan.

America responded to the war with pride and patriotism. Military ranks swelled and troops shipped out to Africa, Europe, and the Pacific theatre. Allied with England, Russia, and others against Japan and Germany, United States' troops spent four long years fighting on foreign soil.

Medical advances allowed the allied armies to receive better medical treatment than their predecessors who fought in World War I. Antibiotics helped control infection and disease, while blood plasma sustained life. Prevention of disease was enhanced by the use of DDT to eliminate vectors carrying malaria and typhus, and soldiers were innoculated against yellow fever and tetanus.

Meanwhile at home Americans zealously maintained the war effort. Advanced technology made this conflict dependent upon industry, and incredible amounts of materials were required to equip the armies with food, shelter, weapons, medical supplies, and transportation. Expanded factories employed thousands of workers needed to produce the necessary war goods. Nothing was too much for the cause and citizens dutifully accepted the rationing of gasoline, tires, and some foods while waiting for the war to end.

Nearly every ablebodied man was serving in the military, and others worked in industry. Women filled the labor force taking jobs in factories and with civilian defense. Hospitals suffered grievous loss of manpower directly to the war and also to industry. Many institutions had difficulty caring for patients and even staying open. Shortages of doctors, nurses, and all other workers made the delivery of health care nearly impossible, and much of the work now fell to the students in the nursing schools. Under the auspices of the American Red Cross and the Office of Civilian Defense, programs were set up across the country to train volunteer nurses' aides. The work of these women was of great benefit, and it is difficult to imagine how hospital work could have been carried on without these volunteers.

Incredible contributions were made by American nurses during World War II. Demand for their services was unprecedented and for the first time federal funds were allocated for the education of nurses. They answered the call and enlisted by the thousands, shipping off to Europe, Africa, and Asia, as well as working on the home front to staff the military and civilian hospitals.

As the crisis grew the National Nursing Council for War dealt with the supply and demand of nursing service, helping individual nurses with the decision of whether to enlist or remain in civilian nursing. In 1944 Congress voted to give Army and Navy nurses temporary officer rank with full benefits equal to males of that rank. Nurses worked in the war zones and in other areas, some as flight nurses, a role created by the war. As the fighting continued the need for nurses rose. In January 1945 President Roosevelt asked Congress to pass a bill conscripting nurses and thousands enlisted before action was taken on the bill so that by the end of April there was an excess of military nurses. The bill was not enacted and by late summer the war was over.

The increased supply of nurses for the war effort was in part a direct result of the U.S. Cadet Nurse Corps. Congresswoman Frances Payne Bolton sponsored the bill authorizing the creation of the Corps and it was passed in 1943. Subsidized by the Public Health Service, funds were granted to nursing schools for tuition, fees, books, uniforms, and the stipends of Cadet Nurses. To qualify for the program a student had to be between seventeen and thirty-five years of age, meet all admission requirements, and agree to engage in essential military or civilian nursing for the duration of the war. Nursing programs were shortened for the basic educational program, then for the last six or twelve months before graduation the Senior Cadet Nurse could choose assignment in another civilian, government, or military institution or remain at the home hospital.

The Cadet program attracted thousands of young women. The accelerated program enabled them to assume positions of responsibility earlier, thus benefitting the war effort. They received the same education as other students and while on duty wore the uniform of the school with a Cadet Corps patch. Off duty they could wear the uniform of the Corps. A student's entire education was paid for in exchange for her commitment to work in nursing for the remainder of the war. When the war ended those already enrolled in the program were assured of the benefits until graduation. In 1948 the last of the Cadet Corps Nurses were graduated making a total of 125,000 registered nurses who had been members of the U.S. Cadet Corps.

Nursing was keenly affected by World War II but the declaration of peace on September 2, 1945, in no way lessened the demand for nurses. The shortage remained serious as low wages and unpleasant working conditions combined with unfair employment practices by some hospitals continued to discourage nurses.

After 1945 applications to schools of nursing decreased and the withdrawal of enrolled students was high. Nursing's popularity decreased as other careers offered more advantages. Also a bitter controversy had begun over the collegiate preparation of nurses. Critical viewpoints were expressed by many non-nurses (especially members of the American Medical Association and the American Hospital Association), but nurse educators defended their position. By mid-century there were approximately one hundred and fifty college programs for nursing education.

In 1948 a study by Esther Lucile Brown recommended that schools be forced to upgrade their standards, that state boards enforce them, and that the public be asked to assume part of the financial responsibility of nursing education. Another study of that time suggested that professional nurses complete a four-year course of study at a college or university.

Simultaneously, the stratification of nursing offered some relief to the vast shortages. "Practical nurse" became a sanctioned term, and these nurses could care for patients under the direct supervision of a physician or registered nurse, while nurses aides could give unskilled care. The nursing team with its different levels of personnel developed from this point. By 1950 the profession had achieved some of its early goals and was setting new ones.

The Hospital

As the decade began the hospital needed repairs, renovations, and expansion. Certain measures were taken to allow for a more moderate traffic flow through the corridors and this helped decrease travel in the rotunda area, while new equipment eased work in the kitchen and X-ray departments. When war was declared plans for enlargement were delayed and no major modernizations took place for several years as materials and labor were channeled into the war effort.

Several changes took place during the 1940s. In 1940 the Trustees accepted Miss Griffin's resignation. This untoward happening disturbed many as she had guided the school through stressful times and pursued the highest standards of nursing and nursing education. Donald Smith, then superintendent of the hospital wrote, "During her incumbency definite progress was made in nursing education in this school, and it became even more widely and favorably known." Miss Cecilia H. Schaefer, R.N. (MHMH Class of 1933), the obstetrical supervisor, was named Acting Superintendent of Nurses and Principal of the School of Nursing. She carried out these duties quite effectively, and in 1941 Miss Marie V. Dowler, R.N. was appointed to that dual position. Miss Dowler was well qualified for the job and she directed the work of the school and hospital nursing service for the next ten years.

Donald Smith was forced to take a year's leave of absence from the superintendent's position in 1944 and until his return in 1945 James W. Campion, Jr. took over the post. In 1947 Mr. Smith died and the position was turned over to the assistant superintendent, Harold A. Callahan. In 1948 William L. Wilson joined the Mary Hitchcock Hospital as administrator and he enjoyed a long and fruitful term until his retirement in 1978.

War conditions were much in evidence at the hospital. Shortages were felt as imposed rationing limited some foods as well as supplies of drugs and equipment. Metal and rubber were all but unobtainable and personnel had to find substitutes for many everyday goods.

As staff members were released for war service those remaining at the hospital assumed more duties and longer hours. Hospital use increased and the average daily patient census rose. Some departments operated with only 50 percent of their usual staff and persons were shifted from one department to another in order to share the workload. Nurses were especially burdened and they performed many duties in addition to nursing.

The hospital might not have continued its efficient service without the valiant efforts of many volunteers. In 1941 two instructors at the nursing school taught a Red Cross nurses' aide course to area women. These enthusiastic students later rendered invaluable assistance to the overworked nurses at the hospital and they staffed the temporary infirmaries during the influenza and measle epidemics of 1942 and 1943.

The Mary Hitchcock Auxiliary also made great contributions and members gave countless hours of volunteer service as they distributed reading materials, comforted patients, and gave assistance where they could. The group also conducted their usual fund-raising activities with much success. Their spirit and energy were fine examples to all.

Other citizens also came to the aid of Mary Hitchcock. Many were at the hospital three times a day to help pass trays, wash dishes as well as clean and scrub floors. Enough cannot be written in appreciation of all who volunteered their services during those difficult times.

The hospital participated in various national programs to support the war. In 1943 a blood and plasma bank was established for both civilian and military needs. Mary Hitchcock also contracted with the federal government to participate as a member of the U.S. Cadet Nurse Corps program.

When peace was finally declared, the trustees again analyzed the long-range expansion of the hospital. In 1945 they authorized the construction of the Winifred S. Raven Convalescent Unit, the gift of Professor Anton A. Raven in memory of his wife, and the facility opened in July 1947. That same year it was announced that Mrs. Edward D. Faulkner, of Woodstock, Vermont, intended making a very large gift for the hospital's major expansion project. The need for nurses' housing was urgent and in 1949 work began on a new nurses' residence.

In the postwar period much thought was given to the nursing needs of Mary Hitchcock. The demand for nursing service was great and would increase with the proposed enlargement. After the war the number of volunteers had decreased but the need for their services had not. Therefore in 1946 a group of Senior Girl Scouts was trained to assist nurses with clerical and miscellaneous duties, but this was not a long-term solution. It was obvious that shorter hours, better working conditions, and the use of ancillary personnel were necessary. The call for private duty nurses did not regain its pre-depression level and more graduate nurses began to turn to hospital and other types of nursing.*

The School Of Nursing

The school of nursing was in desperate need of expansion. The living quarters of Billings-Lee and the '37 Building housed many more students than were intended. In fact, in 1940 when the Nursing Council on National Defense requested schools to increase their enrollment, Mary Hitchcock could not comply as the school was hard pressed to admit enough students to meet present hospital demands. However, two years later, in 1942, the Patten House on Webster Avenue was leased to provide accommodations for students and the school was able to respond to the council's appeal.

When physical expansion was not feasible renovations and repairs did much to enhance the school's existing facilities. The library, though catalogued, had long needed attention. In 1941 it was refurbished with adequate lighting and seating; file cabinets, a magazine rack, and a large study table were installed. Classrooms were also improved at that time, and in 1944 the purchase of more modern teaching aids reinforced the classroom instruction received by the students.

Building projects were deferred during the war but at the end of the decade construction began on the long-planned school expansion. The '50 Building would afford the space and amenities which the school needed.

By 1940 the ward teaching program had become more formally organized. The physicians, nurses, and (occasionally) students prepared and conducted clinics, lectures, and demonstrations on the hospital wards. However, as the hospital lost great numbers of personnel to the war service this teaching method became irregular and difficult to administer.

* Some nurses remained in the service after the war and others explored the expanding fields of public health, school nursing, and industrial nursing. A number of the Mary Hitchcock graduates were attracted to the hospital's School of Anesthesia Technology which opened in 1943.

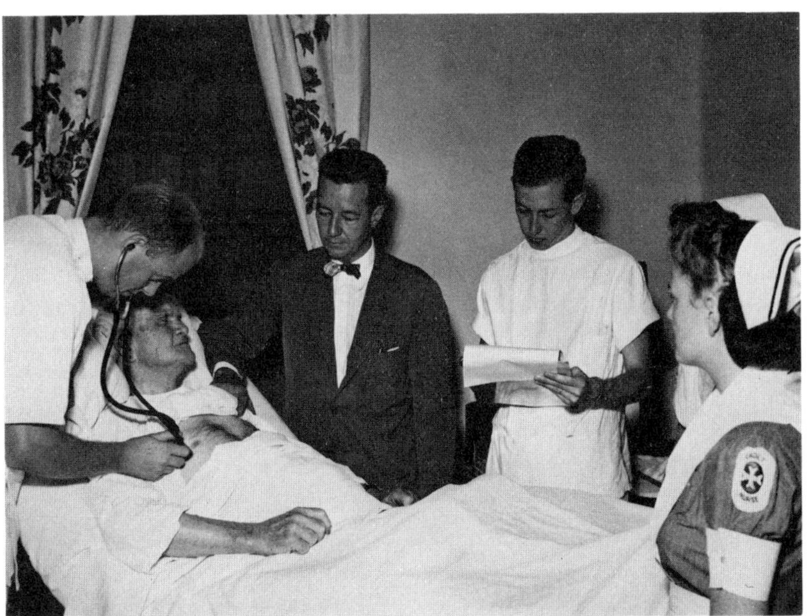

During World War II students in the U.S. Cadet Corps Training program wore the school uniform with the patch of the Corps.

Several changes and additions were made in the clinical aspect of the school's educational program. In 1940 Miss Schaefer helped institute a one-month rotation at the Hitchcock Clinic. Here students worked with the clinic nurses and learned the rudiments of outpatient nursing while the clinic physicians taught medical aspects of such treatment.

In 1942 an assistant to the nursing arts instructor was hired and the preclinical term was increased from sixteen to twenty weeks to allow for a longer adjustment period. The hours of hospital service by preclinical students were decreased also. These progressive changes were short-lived however, and in 1945 the preclinical period was reduced to sixteen weeks.

An important and long-needed addition to the curriculum was made in 1944 when the school began its affiliate program in psychiatric nursing. Mary Hitchcock students had suffered from the lack of such an experience by not qualifying for certain nursing positions. Now with 63 percent of the war casualties requiring some type of psychiatric care it was imperative that such a course be adopted. In December 1944 the first group of students went to the New Hampshire Hospital in Concord for three months where they worked on the clinical units and received instruction from the faculty of that school of nursing. Every three months a new group was sent for the affiliation.

The effects of the war were felt by nearly everyone. At the hospital patients gracefully accepted limitations due to the shortage of manpower. At times they cheerfully helped the nurses and each other. If volunteer help was reduced on a particular day, Miss Dowler and the supervisors rolled up their sleeves and washed dishes. A student nurse worked very hard, often doing the tasks normally assigned to several persons. Everyone pitched in and gave help where it was needed. Crowded conditions meant more work, but the morale was high and the standards of Mary Hitchcock were maintained as much as was humanly possible.

Eager to assist the government in the training of qualified nurses the Mary Hitchcock School of Nursing became a member of the U.S. Cadet Corps Program. When the Corps was instituted there 98.5 percent of the eligible students enrolled. The school quickly accepted a third class in 1943 and by 1944 there were 116 students at Mary Hitchcock. Max Norton, president of the hospital wrote: "We are pleased . . . that we can be a contributor to the war effort in the all important work of procurement and training of nurses."

In Miss Dowler's administration of the school she endeavored to obtain shorter hours, better educational programs, and improved recreational opportunities for the students. In 1942 the students were working longer hours than recommended by the state board, but gradually these were reduced and a better balance was achieved. The eight-hour day for students which already had begun for those on night duty on three wards, was eventually incorporated and adequate hospital coverage maintained.

Throughout these busy years the hospital physicians were kind and understanding in their relationships with the students. They appreciated the problems faced by the nurses in coping with increased work and fewer helpers. They continued to lecture to classes when time permitted and made every effort to contribute to the education of the nurses.

The postwar appraisal of nursing and nursing education on a national level was carried out at Mary Hitchcock, also faculty worked hard to advance nursing and students were even more carefully selected than in previous times. Faculty and students worked together for higher achievement at the school and as they approached mid-century, the school's educational program was well-planned and implemented to prepare nurses for their new roles ahead.

10

Students And The War

THE NUMBER of applicants to the Mary Hitchcock School of Nursing increased after the start of the war. The Cadet Corps offered attractive benefits and many young women took advantage of the opportunities created. Although the war effort inspired some to apply others would have sought to become nurses anyway.

Most of the new students entering Mary Hitchcock did not know anyone there and arrived feeling confused, bewildered, and excited. A well organized "Big Sister" program made the adjustment to nursing school easier. Each probationer was assigned to an upperclassman who greeted her, explained rules, and generally advised her on life at Mary Hitchcock. Probationers were usually assigned to Patten House, where on their first day they met roommates and classmates, and put away their clothes. Later in the day a tea, or reception, provided the opportunity to meet school personnel and faculty. Students received basic information about the school and were shown around so that by evening they were usually more comfortable with the physical surroundings and had been reassured that it was usual to feel nervous.

The Senior Sister assigned to the class was an important person in the lives of the probationers. She provided encouragement and support as she worked with them in the classroom and on the wards. She was nearly always available to answer questions, and in her off-duty time she tutored those who needed extra help. The Senior Sister was dedicated to helping these students become nurses.

The school's basketball team and coach, 1944.

At the beginning of the 1940s the student nurses worked nearly as many hours as their predecessors. Miss Dowler and her staff gradually made a significant reduction in the number of student service hours. It was a process which took careful planning and implementation. Over a period of several years a much more balanced program was achieved. By the end of the decade students had a schedule which allowed for study, rest, and recreation, as well as more consistent days off. This was all achieved without compromising service to the hospital.

Students still rotated to the various hospital units and supplied the hospital's night nursing. The war shortages of personnel made extra work and the hospital was sometimes so crowded that a nurse could scarcely squeeze between beds in a ward. The students found themselves with large patient assignments that sometimes seemed impossible to complete. No one could bathe, feed, and make beds for nine patients in two and a half hours!

The nurses often had chores that took them away from nursing duties. Even with volunteer help there were not enough workers to do the job and the problems persisted. In 1945 Miss Dowler remarked, "...

Patients sometimes go without prompt and thorough care because the nurse is occupied with essential non-nursing duties which should be delegated to a ward helper." Despite the pressures to accomplish so much the nurses and workers were cheerful and tackled their jobs with vigor.

Psychiatric nursing was undoubtedly the most often discussed course. Girls returning from the affiliated institution spoke with strange words about nursing situations unheard of in Hanover. The novelty of attending another school for three months plus the intrigue of psychiatry provided the students with something to anticipate and dread at the same time.

The students were used to the compact wards and buildings of Mary Hitchcock, and the New Hampshire Hospital seemed like a sprawling giant with its many buildings and wards. It took time to learn one's way around, and the unfamiliar practice of carrying keys to the locked wards was disconcerting to some. A few of the students enjoyed this new kind of nursing and were quite comfortable with it; others could barely wait for the return to Mary Hitchcock.

When the students were not working much of their time was spent in or near the residences where they lived. Dormitory life, monitored by housemothers, was generally pleasant and the girls passed time playing bridge, sunning on the roof of '37 Building, listening to music, or just being together. In back of the school a Victory Garden gave the girls a chance to use their gardening skills and reap the benefits.

In the summer baseball games and picnics provided entertainment and the girls frequently rode the bicycles which had been given to the school by the clinic physicians. The school's basketball team took on challengers during the winter, and movies, dances, and concerts were always popular.

There were plenty of chances to socialize with other young people and the students enjoyed parties and dances with the young servicemen living in Hanover and the students of the medical school and college. Several of these parties were held at the nursing school while some were at the college. The controversial issue of students being prohibited from entering fraternities was debated during this time and finally the ban was lifted.

In 1945 the first issue of the school newspaper appeared, and for several years students and other personnel were kept abreast of the "news" of Mary Hitchcock. Early issues of the paper featured letters from the hospital staff in the service. Of special interest to the students were those letters from school alumnae who were nursing for the military.

The student government had its beginnings during these years and the students were sincere in their efforts to upgrade achievement and work for the betterment of the school. This organization would continue to develop and play an important part in student life in the years to come.

For some years the students had wished to wear white shoes and stockings with the school uniform instead of the black ones. This fashion had previously been reserved for graduates. The school personnel did not endorse the change for some time but finally the Senior Nurses were awarded the privilege. The underclassmen were so eager for the same liberty that they volunteered to wash stockings and polish shoes for the seniors! Eventually the entire student body was permitted to wear white accessories and they became a standard part of the uniform.

The nurses faced not only the daily challenges of work and study but many of them had families and friends overseas. The war took on special meaning for them and they often made a special effort at Mary Hitchcock. It is interesting to note that the majority of Senior Cadet Nurses chose to remain at Mary Hitchcock for the last six months of school. The hospital was well served by its students at a difficult time.

Part 3

Maturity

11

A Time Of Change

BETWEEN 1950 and 1965 the very foundations of American society were shaken as dramatic changes spread throughout the country. Citizens found their lives affected by advancing technology, political aberrations, United States war involvement, and grave social issues which required large adjustments within a short period.

Technology brought the freedom of convenience living as city dwellers moved to the suburbs and rural citizens moved off the farm. Americans used modern appliances, drove fast cars, and watched television while the Atomic Age gave way to the Space Age.

Medicine continued its development to new levels of sophistication. Polio vaccine rendered the iron lung all but unnecessary: psychotropic drugs altered the psychotic behavior of the emotionally ill, and unprecedented surgical techniques repaired vital organs. Medical science, technology, and ongoing research brought daily hope for cures of major diseases.

This period saw the dramatic growth of American psychiatry. Specialization within that field brought new understanding of emotional disorders and the public was helped to learn more about mental illness. In the early and mid-1960s the traditional modalities of psychiatric treatment were abandoned as the community mental health movement got underway, and the stigma of mental illness was slowly cast aside.

As the nursing profession came to the mid-century point the demand for qualified nurses was great, but the serious shortage of the postwar years persisted. Many new hospitals and health care facilities were constructed but often there were not enough nurses to staff them. More programs were started to train auxiliary workers thus freeing nurses to attend to the nursing duties for which they were educated. At the same time minority groups within the profession began to assert themselves and nursing schools and hospitals reexamined their admission and personnel policies.

The Korean War required large numbers of nurses and new roles for these nurses were created. The Air Force Nurse Corps was established and for the first time nurses participated in air evacuation programs.

Psychiatric nursing developed along with the growth of psychiatry. Schools of nursing increased the amount of theory and practice students received and gradually more nurses looked toward a career in the nursing of emotionally ill patients. One entire section of the State Board Examination for licensure was devoted to psychiatric nursing.

Nursing Education Is Reexamined

Two major issues of that time with which the profession dealt were reorganization and accreditation. Nurses realized the need for both and organization was greatly simplified in 1950 when the six national nursing associations united and distributed their membership into two groups: The American Nurses' Association (ANA), and the National League for Nursing (NLN). These two bodies have functioned competently and better serve the professional needs of nurses.

Accreditation, long deemed necessary, had been an informal practice at best. In 1952 the NLN assumed official responsibility for it when the Temporary Accrediting Service was established. A five-year project was carried out to survey and "accredit" those schools meeting certain minimum standards. In 1952 the list of schools given the temporary accreditation was published in the *American Journal of Nursing*. This list represented both diploma and degree programs and by 1958 the majority of the schools had achieved full accreditation status. Most had upgraded their educational programs and were in favor of continual review and efforts to refine the educational process. Those schools which did not meet the standards closed, or in some cases, continued as non-accredited institutions. The public had access then, as it does today, to lists of NLN accredited schools of nursing.

The State Board Test Pool, begun in 1944 with only six states, realized full national participation in 1950 when every state had adopted the pool. For the first time licensing examinations were standardized throughout the country. Each state, however, set its own acceptable score for licensure.

In 1952 the world of nursing education received another jolt when Dr. Mildred Montag, R.N. proposed a concept of nursing education which would educate nurses in a two-year community or junior college and prepare them as bedside nurses while they earned an associate degree. Many educators and others were unconvinced that this type of program could work, but in 1958 the results of a five-year study declared that it was indeed possible to prepare nurses in this fashion, and furthermore these beginning practitioners did as well on state board examinations as those from other types of schools.

Proponents of the diploma schools argued that the three year nurses were better "qualified" to give nursing care and that they had more clinical experience. Advocates of the associate degree programs pointed to cost factors and hospital administrators had to admit that in most cases their schools cost more to operate than the students paid in tuition and fees. The associate degree programs could finance nursing education as any other college program was funded, often receiving state or federal monies. The debate went on, but farsighted leaders of nursing looked ahead with the knowledge that ultimately the goal was to educate nurses on the baccalaureate level within the general system of education. Still, the furor rose and was heard nationwide as the diploma school was being threatened.

The total number of nursing schools in the United States was declining, but the number of baccalaureate programs was increasing. These programs were still of highly variable quality, but the continued accreditation program helped all schools to look closely at their curriculums and as the science of nursing became more precise, the need for more highly qualified faculty on all levels grew. By 1960 diploma education had improved greatly and the majority of nurses was still educated in the hospital schools. The 1960s brought more baccalaureate and graduate nursing programs, and the longtime shortage of nurses began to lessen.

Within this fifteen year period many legislative measures were passed which provided funding for nursing education. Some money was allocated for undergraduate study while other legislation enabled registered nurses to study nursing administration, supervision, and education. In 1964 the Nurse Training Act provided for loans, scholarships, and traineeships for advanced study.

In 1960 the ANA held its forty-second national convention, and a report was given on the long term goals for nursing. At that time "Goal Three" projected the necessity of baccalaureate preparation for nurses "within the next twenty to thirty years." It was clarified that the ANA would support the baccalaureate programs as the basic preparation for nurses when that necessity was realized.

Then, in December, 1965, the ANA Committee on Education prepared a position paper which was adopted by the association's board of directors. The controversial ANA Position Paper on Education for Nursing stated:

1. Nursing education should take place in institutions of higher learning.
2. The minimum preparation for professional nurses should be a baccalaureate degree.
3. The minimum preparation for technical nurses should be an associate degree.
4. Nursing assistants should receive intensive vocational education programs.

The diploma programs were not mentioned in the paper and the antagonism which had been smoldering for years flared and the dissension between types of nursing programs increased. Supporters of each group argued that their preference was the best, and nursing education became more perplexing to the prospective student and to the general public. Nursing educators, nurses, and nursing students were forced to look to the future and make decisions regarding the profession and themselves.

Since 1947 a five-nurse board had been legally responsible for setting the standards of nursing education and the licensure of nurses in New Hampshire. In 1955 the Board of Nurse Examiners changed its name to the Board of Nursing Education and Nurse Registration. This body was very effective in raising the standards of nursing and nursing education in New Hampshire, and in a manner similar to that of the NLN the state board also approved or accredited schools within the state. A state accredited school met the criteria deemed acceptable by the board and was periodically visited to ensure maintenance of standards.

By 1950 New Hampshire schools were required to teach psychiatric nursing, as well as to maintain contractual agreements with any affiliate school where students received instruction. New Hampshire had first used the national licensing examination in 1947, and by 1950 there was a 24 percent reduction in first-time failures.

Money was allocated for state aid for nursing education in 1957 when the first state scholarship program was initiated. State programs of this nature continued and several amendments to the New Hampshire nurse practice act provided funding for education.

Although nurses had to be registered in the state for many years it was not until 1959 that New Hampshire required all professional nurses who practice nursing for hire to be licensed.* Similar legislation for practical nurses was enacted in 1965.

The progress of American nursing was paralleled by the growth of nursing in New Hampshire. The New Hampshire State Nurses Association (NHSNA), the professional forum for the state's nurses, remained active in the affairs of the ANA and was instrumental in achieving nursing legislation in New Hampshire. In 1954 the association received a grant for a study of nursing functions which prompted the later allocations of state aid for nursing education.

The Hospital

The hospital's physical conditions were in a state of decline when Mr. Wilson began his administration in 1948, since only minimal repairs and upkeep were possible during World War II. Wards were run down and crowded and some of the equipment was wearing out. Attention to buildings and equipment was authorized and organizational changes were made which contributed to the hospital's operating efficiency. These measures helped ready the hospital for expansion and growth.

Since the hospital had continued to provide more service, wards were crowded. In addition nursing personnel were in short supply so that more nurses' aides were introduced on a salaried basis. Orderlies and technicians were also employed.

In 1950 the cornerstone for the new Faulkner addition was laid. Hospital personnel looked forward to its completion with anticipation. That same year a public address system serving the hospital, Dick Hall's House, the Clinic, and the Winifred Raven House was installed. Meanwhile costs were rising and the administration worried about expenses. In 1952 it was noted in a pamphlet titled "A New Era of Service" published by the hospital that the school of nursing was a financial concern in that its expenses exceeded the tuition received from its students.

* In 1939 New York became the first state requiring nurses to be licensed in order to practice professional nursing.

On February 2, 1952, the dedication ceremonies were held for the Faulkner Building. The donor, Mrs. Marianne G. Faulkner, was the guest of honor and an open house was held. The new building housed modern patient care units, eight operating rooms, plenty of space for new departments and an attractive lobby. The building was occupied the following summer when a systematic plan was implemented to move patients and entire departments from the older hospital areas into the new "Faulkner House." The first ward clerks were employed at this time and they were welcomed by other personnel as they answered the telephones, did some of the paperwork, and took on many miscellaneous duties.

These years brought many changes in administrative nursing personnel at Mary Hitchcock, some due to the reorganization of the hospital's nursing department as it became more complex. Miss Dowler, after eleven years of excellent leadership, resigned in 1951 and was succeeded as the Director of Nursing Service and Nursing Education by Miss Mary Louise Fernald. Miss Fernald brought to the position both expertise and energy. During her term the dual role was separated into two positions and in 1957 Miss Fernald retained the title of Director of Nursing Education while Mrs. Elizabeth (Bowles) Ward (MHMH Class of 1945) and Miss Alice Straw (MHMH Class of 1944) became Acting Directors of Nursing Service. In 1958 Miss Irja Hill, prepared in nursing service administration, was appointed to fill the position of Director of Nursing Service, a title she held for nine years. In 1960, after Miss Fernald's resignation, Mrs. Katherine Schenk became the Director of Nursing Education.

Changes came quickly in these years. In 1953 the hospital established the forty-hour work week (which coupled with acceptable wages made the hospital competitive in the local labor market); in 1955 the first television set was installed in the children's unit; and 1957 brought the reorganization of the department of nursing.

Professional advances included the establishment of the hospital's first Special Care Unit in 1955. Both nurses and physicians urged the formation of a designated area to care for the critically ill, and their efforts resulted in the conversion of the old A ward to such a unit. This type of critical care unit was one of the earliest in the country. Before the discovery of the Salk polio vaccine the B Ward was set up with respirators and other equipment to care for polio victims. By grouping patients with similar diseases hospital personnel could provide more efficient, expert, and complete care.

In the early 1960s Civil Defense was a major consideration in overall planning at Mary Hitchcock and personnel were instructed in specific measures in case of nuclear attack. In 1962 the auxiliary of the hospital began to staff the information desk with volunteers, and they introduced their junior volunteer program, the Candy Stripers, into the hospital.

Although the hospital attracted many workers, a persistent difficulty had been the maintenance of an adequate supply of qualified registered nurses. In 1958 it was noted that for the first time in several years all the budgeted positions for nurses were filled. This was becoming even more important as the school of nursing was decreasing its students' hours of hospital service as it emphasized the educational program.

Team nursing was developed at the hospital and additional specialized units came into being. Gradually Mary Hitchcock attracted more nurses who had graduated from other schools of nursing. For many years the great majority of nurses had been its own graduates, but now as changes occurred other people came with new ideas and different ways of doing things. As the nursing service adapted to the many changes at Mary Hitchcock the hospital and nursing administrations considered the future nursing needs of the facility.*

The School Of Nursing

The long-awaited addition to the school of nursing was completed in 1950. The new building not only offered relief from the cramped living quarters but provided space for much-needed classrooms, offices, and a library. The school acquired its first science laboratory at that time, having previously used facilities at Dartmouth College or the medical school. The modern, well-constructed building was most welcome to all the school personnel and students.

The additional physical space permitted the school's enrollment to be increased as the hospital expanded. An active recruitment program was begun and in 1952 the school organized and published a school bulletin. In September of that year a record class of sixty-two preclinical students entered the school. During the next few years successful attempts were made to reduce the school's high attrition rate which at

* Team nursing was a national trend implemented to meet the demand for organized nursing care.

First year students, 1952. By the early 1950s classes were admitted once a year.

times ran over 30 percent in a given class.* Meanwhile recruitment efforts were maintained and during that time faculty and other school representatives went into Hanover and nearby communities to talk about nursing education and answer the questions of interested persons.

In 1951 the School of Nursing Advisory Committee was established. The membership of this group was composed of representatives from the school, hospital, hospital auxiliary, medical school, secondary public schools, and the community. This body acted in an advisory capacity to the school by interpreting the school's needs and objectives to the board of trustees, by interpreting certain policies to the faculty of the nursing school, by acting as a liaison between the school and community, and by assisting in the planning and development of educational and recreational opportunities for students of the school. The committee also helped facilitate action on the recommendations made by the school's director. Members of the committee were appointed for specific terms by the board of trustees. This committee functioned until 1976 when it was dissolved.

The director of nursing education was assisted in the management of the school's affairs by an educational director, who was a full-time faculty member. This position gradually evolved into that of associate director a few years after the division of nursing service and education was established in 1957.

The school of nursing was growing and its staff increased. Also when the new Faulkner units were opened the hospital increased the number of its employees. In 1952 the annual report of the school to the New Hampshire Board of Nurse Examiners listed the numbers of professional staff as follows:

Director Nursing Service / Education	1
Educational Director (instructor)	1
Instructors	5
Assistant Directors Nursing Service	3
Health Director	1
Nursing Supervisors	7
Head nurses	11
Staff nurses	32
Suture nurses	6
Nutrition / cookery instructions	2
Social Service director	1

* Classes were now admitted once a year, in the fall.

There were also nurses' aides, orderlies, and technicians employed in the hospital at this time.

The Upper Valley's transient population as well as its geographical location often made it difficult to retain qualified faculty at the school. Recruitment was a problem and Miss Fernald noted that at times faculty members carried "tremendous loads." Nevertheless they were a dedicated and industrious group as they undertook the development of the Division of Nursing Education and the strengthening of the school's curriculum. The instructors were adamant about maintaining high educational standards and insisted that the school seek NLN accreditation.

In 1952 the Mary Hitchcock Memorial Hospital School of Nursing received temporary accreditation from the NLN and was on the published list of schools holding that status. Miss Fernald and the faculty began to review and redefine the school's objectives, philosophy, and evaluation methods in preparation for the next accreditation visit in 1957. They spent much time and effort on the task and in 1958 the school was given full accreditation for five years. The Mary Hitchcock school was one of the first two schools in New Hampshire to have this distinction.

During the years of revision and examination of the school's educational program the faculty met regularly, often in the evening after a long day's work. In 1954 Miss Fernald reported that the school showed educational progress. Committees were established and worked on specific goals, while course outlines, clinical instruction, and the entire curriculum were continually reviewed and rewritten.

The division of the nursing service and nursing education departments came about after careful study. Both service and education had become increasingly complex and each constituency needed full-time direction. Miss Fernald was pleased with the reorganization and was able to devote more time and energy to furthering the work of the school after the departmental separation. She continued to work very closely with the nursing service personnel and in 1958 wrote " . . . It is only by working together that we will improve the education of nurses and the nursing care of patients."

The new Faulkner units provided excellent clinical facilities where the students gained valuable experience. As more instructors were hired the supervision was improved and the entire teaching responsibility gradually was turned over to school personnel. (For years supervisors had taken some of that responsibility.)

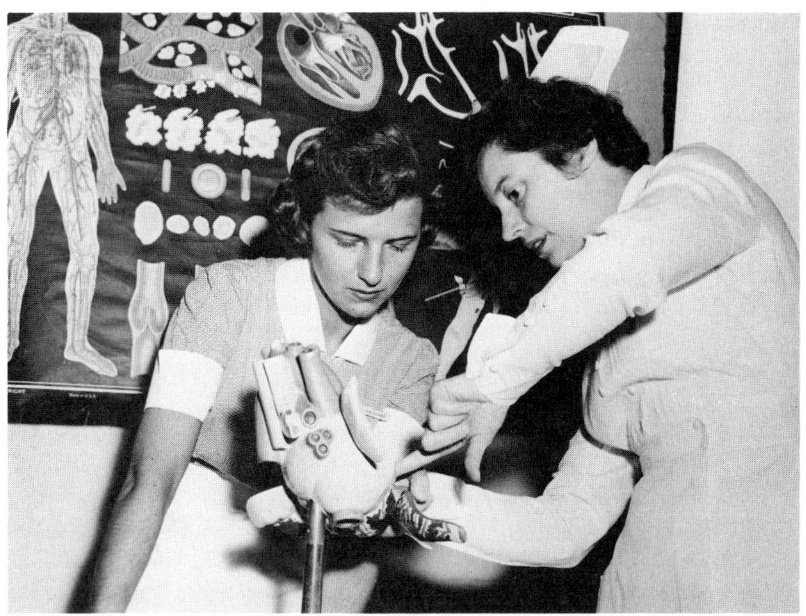

The educational program was strengthened materially during the 1950s and early 1960s.

In 1955 the school began an affiliation in obstetrical nursing with the school at the Boston Lying-In Hospital. The students went there for three months while they received theoretical and clinical instruction. In 1956 a similar program was arranged with the Boston Children's Hospital. The pediatric nursing rotation, which had been of concern for so long, was now held at one of the finest centers for the care of children. These two clinical affiliations provided expanded learning opportunities for the students of Mary Hitchcock.*

The first guidance counselor came to the school in 1954 and she offered valuable services to the students. A student/faculty committee began a library for recreational reading in order to widen the scope of student interests. Instructors and students enjoyed working together on this project. Meanwhile the addition of faculty strengthened the clinical program, and the medical/surgical areas of the curriculum were broadened. During these years the first exploratory dialogue was

* At this time many nursing schools utilized affiliate programs to insure enriched clinical experience in specialized areas of nursing. Usually students were exposed to a greater variety of experiences.

held between Mary Hitchcock's nursing school and other educational facilities as baccalaureate preparation of nurses became a major trend. Also the hospital's continued growth led to speculation about possible changes in nursing education there. Educators at the school and the hospital's administrators felt that it was wise to begin the examination of alternatives.

Some of the students completing the three year program went immediately to college; others took courses from time to time. It was felt that perhaps some credit courses could be built into the school's offerings. Discussions were held with various groups but there were no definitive results.

Miss Fernald served both the hospital and especially the school, as major changes took place and the educational component of nursing education came into important focus. After eight years of dedication to nursing and nursing education at Mary Hitchcock she left the post and was succeeded by Mrs. Katherine Schenk in 1960. Mrs. Schenk, a faculty member for seven years, was comfortable with the school and other members of the faculty and familiar with educational matters.

Mrs. Schenk proved to be a vigorous and able leader. She directed the school through the arduous process of further separation from the nursing service department, a task she accomplished with efficiency and diplomacy. She and Miss Irja Hill, Director of Nursing Service, worked closely in planning the students' clinical experiences while considering the needs of the hospital and its nursing service. It was traditional that students were used as service members, and the change was not easy. Mrs. Schenk encouraged the cooperation of head nurses, supervisors, and instructors, and advised the use of conferences in the clinical areas to plan for good patient care and to work out differences. In her annual report to nursing service in 1962 she wrote " . . . We all know that the objectives of the school, must, in many cases, conflict with the needs of the Nursing Service Department." With concern for the nursing care received by patients, and the educational needs of the students in mind, Mrs. Schenk and Miss Hill worked out the gradual implementation of a plan to decrease the hospital's dependence on the services of the students. In 1964 Miss Hill wrote, "In the past several years our school of nursing has been changing to an education-centered program." This clearly defined the direction of the nursing education at the school and by the fall of 1965 it was generally acknowledged and accepted that students were not expected to replace the services of employed nursing personnel. The school's tuition and fees were raised as more personnel were hired in lieu of students' services.

The Mary Hitchcock students' expenses were now comparable to those of students in other types of educational programs.

In 1962 the obstetric nursing affiliation with Boston Lying-In Hospital was terminated in order to return the students to the Mary Hitchcock Hospital's obstetrical unit where the experience could be educationally controlled. About the same time team nursing was introduced into the clinical requirements for students. Nursing service personnel had been instrumental in initiating this component as the hospital was using this mode of health care delivery. It proved to be of great value to the third year students and most enjoyed the experience.

In 1963 the school was again visited by the NLN for the purpose of accreditation and this time the agency accredited the school for only two years. The Board of Review for Diploma Programs acknowledged the progress the school had achieved during the previous five years, but also indicated that " . . . serious problems and weaknesses exist in regard to faculty personnel; students; curriculum . . . and evaluation of the educational program." A list of some thirty-three recommendations was included in the report and the school was given two years to act upon them. The faculty took on this sizable task in addition to the rigors of teaching. When a revisit was held in 1965 the NLN felt that progress had been made and accreditation was continued, but emphasized the need for continual evaluation and revision.

In 1964 the psychiatric nursing affiliation with the New Hampshire Hospital in Concord was discontinued and the school entered into an arrangement with Danvers State Hospital in Hathorne, Massachusetts.

Changes in nursing education were occurring rapidly and journals and books were full of speculation about the future of nursing. Mrs. Schenk felt that the New England schools were slower to adopt changes and " . . . This is not all bad, we believe, in that we can hopefully avoid some of the mistakes others have made and also profit from successful ideas." Therefore when the ANA Position Paper was first published the reaction at Mary Hitchcock was not as intense as in some areas. That kind of change was "in the future," not now.

From Apprentice To Student

Nursing education at Mary Hitchcock underwent major changes between 1950 and 1965. The emphasis shifted from apprentice to student as the educational process was recognized as the only viable method of nurse preparation. The innovations came about slowly and

Student nurses represented both hospital and school on Memorial Day in 1952.

were sometimes equally difficult for the educators, student nurses, and hospital personnel.

The growth of nursing education was stimulated by the reorganization of the nursing department in 1957 into two separate entities: service and education. The accreditation program also reinforced the educational aspect of nursing.

The new Faulkner building with its expanded clinical facilities offered Mary Hitchcock students challenging and satisfying experiences. Many cases were referred from all over New England and students had opportunities to work with persons suffering from a great variety of illnesses. Well-planned nurses' stations on each floor provided space to attend to charting and other paperwork as well as a place to hold conferences and discuss plans for patient care. Nurses, instructors, students, and others found the nurses' station a pleasing addition to the facilities.

The forty-four hour week for students had been reduced to forty hours and finally even more hours were cut from the schedule. In the 1950s students averaged forty hours each week including classes. In order to meet hospital needs, however, and still conform to acceptable guidelines for student hours, the students often found themselves scheduled to work a "split" shift. This might mean hours like 7:00 A.M. to 9:00 A.M. on duty, off until 1:00 P.M., and returning for the hours between 1:00 P.M. and 7:00 P.M. While these hours did not violate any recommendations for student work, they effectively limited one's activities for the day. (Some hospital personnel, especially dietary, also worked these split hours.)

Weekends were usually alternated, one on and one off. This practice extended well into the 1960s. Instructors and nursing service personnel made out the time schedules and coordinated them as best they could, balancing students and service people. For many of these years the tendency was to give service persons days off when students were assigned to the units.

Summers were spent working on the units five days a week as classes were suspended for these months. Some of the students might have been away on affiliation at the New Hampshire Hospital during the summer, but the Mary Hitchcock Hospital had a nearly full complement of students to work throughout the warm months.

As the school grew more instructors were hired and the supervision improved somewhat. Students still provided service and worked many evenings and nights, however. Miss Fernald and Mrs. Schenk recognized this as contrary to sound educational policy, but such practices could not be changed overnight. Therefore, with careful planning beforehand, nursing education and nursing service worked together to promote the educational system at Mary Hitchcock.

Mary Louise Fernald had refocused the educational program and her successor Katherine Schenk went on to complete the task by strengthening the school's position on that issue. In the early and mid-1960s the students still worked evenings and nights but the school was slowly moving away from the service advantage. Gradually excessive amounts of evening and night duty were eliminated and clinical experiences were planned with the educational benefits in mind. This was a very slow process which took several years and increased hospital expenses as more registered nurses had to be hired to replace the students' services. Miss Hill, Director of Nursing Service, and Mrs. Schenk worked hard to effect these changes, and by the late 1960s the students were looked upon as learners, and as being at the hospital for the purpose of studying nursing.

The student health program was greatly improved from earlier times. A health supervisor was responsible for looking after ill students when they reported to the health clinic and physicians saw them when necessary. Physical examinations were given to students on admission and they were responsible for reporting monthly weights. Students no longer had to make up every day lost to illness because makeup time was now based on individual cases and worked out with instructors and supervisors. One very clear policy existed however, in regard to makeup time: while students were permitted to sunbathe on the roof they were warned against overexposure, and sick time was not given

The school chorus in concert, 1951.

for sunburn! If one lost clinical time for that reason it had to be made up.

In addition to the wide range of clinical experiences received at Mary Hitchcock, students had affiliations at three other schools. For a span of several years student nurses spent a total of nine months away from Hanover studying nursing specialities at other hospital schools. Affiliations were scheduled to take place in the second or early part of the third years.

For many a highlight of the three years was that six-month period in Boston. Three months were spent at each of two hospitals, and they were always consecutive. Some of the girls from Mary Hitchcock were not accustomed to living in large cities and found it a great adjustment. For others it was an exciting experience and the time passed quickly.

The Boston Lying-In Hospital afforded extensive and varied clinical experiences in the area of obstetrical nursing. Here the students worked with mothers and newborns in a multitude of situations. The work was exacting and sometimes students found it difficult; night duty was a requirement of that program. Nevertheless new friendships were formed and students found time to explore the city.

The Childrens Hospital experience was also challenging. Here the nurses encountered both joy and sadness as they cared for children who had a variety of illnesses. Also valuable training was gained by working with the families of the patients. The daily formal tea held by the Ladies Auxiliary was an event many students of that time remember today.

In 1964 the Mary Hitchcock students affiliated at the Danvers State Hospital. Here they studied emotional illness and cared for the patients on several wards. For many this rotation seemed the longest, and most of them came back "home" to Hanover on the weekends. Although the work was depressing at times, the students made good grades and that school was pleased to have them as affiliates.

During each affiliation a representative of the Mary Hitchcock school visited the students and met with members of the other faculty. Often the director herself would make the trip and these visits were always looked forward to as the students were eager to see someone from home and catch up on the news. Also, the faculty usually sent a package of food and "goodies" from the hospital kitchen.

After the opening of the '50 Building students studying nutrition had weekly labs in cooking where they learned the basics of cookery. These labs were held in the subbasement of the new building off in a small, dark room. They also spent six weeks in the diet kitchen where they prepared the special diets, baked salt-free bread and birthday cakes for patients. They also assisted the dietitian in serving the trays for patients with special dietary needs. On the dietitians' weekends off a student was in charge of the "D.K."

New curriculum guidelines for diploma schools required that behavioral sciences be incorporated into the program. For several years the Mary Hitchcock students had the benefit of instruction from professors of Dartmouth College. Human relations as applied to nursing were also taught, usually by one of the instructors at the school. These sciences were an important element in the humanistic part of nursing and helped prepare the students for a variety of situations which demanded such understanding. In the early 1960s the school added a course in English literature in the hope of stimulating further self-directed thinking. None of these courses provided students with college credits but they enhanced the overall nursing education at the school.

Dormitory life at Mary Hitchcock had evolved into a system of community living which was primarily self-governed by the students. Each student was responsible for her own behavior and she was expected to adhere to the school's honor system of which honesty was the basis.

Classes entered in September each year and new students were warmly greeted by the faculty, housemothers, and the upperclassmen. Every effort was made to put newcomers at ease, and big sisters, housemothers, and faculty were available to help with the adjustment. Homesickness usually passed quickly as students eased into school life.

Each student was assigned a room and was responsible for its tidiness. Regular inspections were conducted by housemothers or designated students, and if a room did not meet standards of cleanliness its occupant received a penalty. Repeated offenses could result in an appearance before the student council.

Each member of the student body belonged to the student government. Meetings were held at regular intervals, and this body (with a faculty advisor) made recommendations for rules and regulations regarding school life. Each class elected officers and a faculty advisor, and directed its own class activities. Representatives were elected to student council, the group which dealt with infractions of rules and other irregularities. For several years there was also a house committee to enforce the dormitory rules and regulations as set forth in a handbook drawn up by a student-faculty group. Each student was expected to read, understand, and comply with the rules.

There were rules and regulations to cover just about every aspect of community living. There were specific times for lights out at night, late permissions, and study hours. These rules were changed as the general societal customs became more relaxed, for example the 1950s "study hours" phased into "quiet hours" and students were free to do what they chose at that time as long as some quiet was maintained for those who wished to study.

Students were required to sign out when leaving the residence and in on their return. A special book was reserved for those going to a

During the 1960s dormitory life evolved into a system of community living with the students taking more responsibility for its direction.

fraternity house, and the names of the student, her escort, and destination were to be recorded. Preclinical students were interviewed personally by the school's director before permission was granted to visit a fraternity for the first time. When visiting the fraternities nurses were subject to college rules concerning women visitors.

There were very specific regulations regarding where the students could or could not go while residing at the school. A college dormitory could not be visited unless special permission were obtained, and a 1964 handbook of the school states that students were not permitted to visit any male apartment or rooming house in the Hanover vicinity.

The traditional chapel service was continued through the early 1950s but as times and needs changed it was discontinued. Students were encouraged to attend their choice of religious services and were welcome to participate in church-sponsored fellowship programs.

Privileges were awarded students deserving of them, and a much-looked-forward-to-period was the last six months of school when a student in good standing received "Senior Privileges." This meant the unlimited use of late permissions, and as long as the student remained in good standing she retained these privileges.

By 1964 the honor system and student government had been in effect for a long time, and by then a specific code of required behavior had evolved. Infractions of rules were classed as major or minor offenses and punished accordingly. The student council dealt with the offenders who reported themselves or were reported by another student. Each student was bound by the honor code to report herself if she broke a rule or if she knew that someone had failed to report herself then she was bound to do so.

While it was acknowledged that social drinking might occur away from the school the students were reminded that they were representatives of Mary Hitchcock and professional nursing. Therefore they were expected to use discretion and good judgment and to remain within the bounds of ladylike behavior. The dress code stipulated that students could not wear haircurlers, bathrobes, or "inappropriate" dress to classes, the cafeteria, or the public area of the nurses residence. The Billings-Lee living room was considered a public place and students passing through were expected to be properly attired. In 1961 the student handbook specified "Short shorts are not to be worn outside the nurses' home while college is in session."

Students could be married during the last half of their senior year, but prospective brides were expected to discuss such plans with the director. This regulation was revised by the mid 1960s and in the late 1960s the marriage policy only required that name changes be recorded.

Recreational opportunities and facilities were available in the school and the Hanover community. During the summer there were many school sponsored activities, and the students enjoyed picnics, hiking, softball, and swimming. When not working or studying they also rode bicycles, played tennis, and engaged in that fond pastime of student nurses: sunbathing on the roof.

In the winter ice skating and skiing remained favorites and many of the girls enjoyed the spectator sports offered by the college. Dartmouth made its swimming pool available to the nurses and for several years the Hanover High School reserved its gymnasium one evening a week for the Mary Hitchcock students. There they played basketball and had scrimmages with local high school teams.

Cultural events at Dartmouth College were open to the students and many of them attended the concerts, lectures, and art exhibits. The

Baker and Howe libraries also offered their services to the student nurses.

There was still much off-duty time spent in the dormitories of the school, however. Here the young women engaged in endless hours of gossip, playing cards, and often cooking large group meals in one of the kitchens of the residence. These "feasts" were great fun and provided relief from the hospital cafeteria fare. In addition everyone shared in the activity and sometimes the housemothers joined in.

Although the housemothers supervised the girls, the director of the school lived in the residence until 1960. She had a suite of rooms in Billings-Lee for some years, then in the '50s Building. Her presence required ingenuity from those students who sought to bend the rules a little. The housemothers were kind and interested in the students. They were truly "mothers" away from home and were always available to chat, listen, or advise.

School events ranged from individual class projects to large-scale activities involving the whole student body. Parties were big events and sometimes the men from the college were invited. They in turn shared some of their fraternity activities with the nursing school students. The nursing school had a glee club for many years, well into the 1960s. It was directed by a Dartmouth College professor, Paul Zeller.

The first yearbook had been published by the class(es) of 1947. For several years there were no more such books until the class of 1954 undertook the publication of the *Salus*. Each class thereafter took great pride in putting together their yearbook to document their memories and experiences. Often it took three years to raise funds for the publication and students held food sales, bazaars, opened a school store, and ran other projects to finance the yearbook.

Students could earn spending money by babysitting for area families and many took advantage of this opportunity regularly. The school handbook later published guidelines for this employment along with rates for payment. In addition the hospital offered students opportunities to work a few hours a week as nurses' aides, ward clerks, or patient sitters.

As students found their educational program shifting they also felt the changes in society. The sixties brought in an age of new social responsibilities, and youth in Hanover and elsewhere were eager to test their independence.

12

An Expanded Role

AMERICANS CONTINUED to adapt and adjust to new social mores. Citizens participated on many levels in movements concerning the issues important to them. At the same time new technological methods assisted scientists in the development of multipurpose instruments and machines that performed amazing functions. Space exploration continued and men were sent to the moon.

Medicine had become highly refined. Surgeons could transplant organs and were able to treat disease previously considered hopeless. Research continued to present new theories, drugs, and cures. Sophisticated equipment enabled physicians to monitor bodily functions and added new dimensions to diagnosis and treatment. In some cases persons could be treated before symptoms of a disease process were manifested. Preventive medicine was a major focus of medical practice.

The delivery of health care had become more complex but also more efficient. Health workers in many settings functioned on interdisciplinary teams, sharing their knowledge and expertise. New roles emerged as paraprofessionals were trained and joined other workers in the health care field. Community health programs grew and increased their services. Citizens responded with interest and new awareness by forming councils and resident groups to advise and assist those managing community agencies.

In 1973 the Mary Hitchcock Memorial Hospital became a component of the Dartmouth-Hitchcock Medical Center.

When the ANA and the NLN announced the formation of the National Commission for the Study of Nursing and Nursing Education in the United States in 1967, another extensive examination of the profession was launched. In 1970 that committee published its recommendations, better known as the Lysaught Report. In that publication the members of the committee recommended:

1. That nursing practice be the focus of nursing,
2. That nursing research be expanded and increased,
3. That state committees be established to plan for nursing education, and
4. That committees be established to assist in the definition of medical and nursing roles.

Nursing practice had become more diverse and areas of specialization were developed as nurses concentrated on better ways to provide patient care. Nursing practice moved from the concept of team nursing to total patient care to primary nursing, as nurses sought to better utilize the nursing process. Meanwhile new roles opened for those interested in nursing management, research, and education. The practicing nurse was now offered a wide variety of professional opportunities which emphasized the need for academic preparation in nursing.

Professional recognition of excellence in nursing practice was the objective of the ANA Certification program established in 1968. Nurses had the opportunity to demonstrate personal and professional achievement and to receive professional acknowledgement. Candidates for certification were required to meet rigid criteria and were thoroughly evaluated in all areas of clinical practice. Written examinations were first given in 1974 and the first professional nurses were awarded Certification in Geriatric Nursing. The program was expanded to include other areas of clinical practice.

With the growing acceptance of the women's movement nurses began to examine their status as women and professionals. They organized for support and to decide actions appropriate for certain issues. The strength of their professional state organizations and the ANA helped them resolve some difficult problems. In 1974 nurses obtained the option for the use of collective bargaining after a large group of San Francisco nurses, endorsed by the California Nurses Association, and supported by the ANA went on strike. This unprecedented action generated the addition of amendments to the Taft-Hartley Act providing for the bargaining measure. Nurses have since continued using political action not only for professional gain but also to affect health legislation through the ANA's Nurses for Political Action and later the Nurses' Coalition for Action in Politics (N-CAP).

Educators and nursing leaders, as well as members of the professional organizations continued to emphasize the need to conduct nursing education within the general system of higher education. In 1976 the National Student Nurses' Association passed a resolution supporting baccalaureate education as the basic preparation for nurses, and further suggested a moratorium on opening any new diploma programs or associate degree schools. In addition the students indicated their willingness to work with other groups to secure additional funding for collegiate nursing programs.*

Nurses began to return to school in record numbers. They studied on full and part time schedules as they worked for that baccalaureate or graduate degree. Thousands of nurses attended school, worked as professional nurses, and raised families. Clearly nurses were committed to professionalism within nursing.

* The New Hampshire Student Nurses' Association was formed in 1951.

The progress of American nursing has not been stifled though at times hampered as nurses have established their competence as practitioners. Nursing has emerged as an independent profession, based on scientific principles, ever responsive to the changing needs of society.

The Statewide Interdisciplinary Planning Project for Nursing and Nursing Education (SIPPNNE) was established in New Hampshire in 1974. In 1975 the project's first year report by Teresa Chopoorian and Margaret Craig urged that nursing education in New Hampshire take place in collegiate programs and that a systematic plan coordinate the phasing out of diploma programs in the state.

The Hospital

In response to the increasing health care needs in the Upper Valley area the Mary Hitchcock Memorial Hospital was enlarged and its already wide range of services was expanded. Such growth had been carefully planned and in 1968 the Dartmouth-Hitchcock Mental Health Center was opened and the addition to the Faulkner Building was completed. By 1972 the new units were opened.

The hospital now had 420 beds and multiple specialty units to treat a variety of illnesses. In 1973 Mary Hitchcock became an integral part of the Dartmouth-Hitchcock Medical Center. With the addition of the Norris Cotton Cancer Center the hospital became even more widely recognized.

This growth required additional personnel for each department of the expanded facility. Many more employees were hired and administrative assistants were appointed to supervise the expanding hospital management.

During this time several changes were made in administrative nursing personnel. Miss Alice Straw, Assistant Director of Nursing Service, became the director of that service when Miss Irja Hill resigned. During her four-year term Miss Straw was called upon in 1970 to assume the additional position of Acting Director of the School of Nursing. In 1971 Miss Helen Herbut, Assistant Director of Nursing Service, was appointed to act as the director of nursing service until the hospital welcomed Marilyn P. Prouty as Assistant Administrator for Nursing in 1972. Mrs. Prouty worked with nursing personnel to reorganize the nursing service department with a focus on "participative management," and she introduced expanded nursing roles into the hospital. Clinical specialists with graduate preparation in specialized

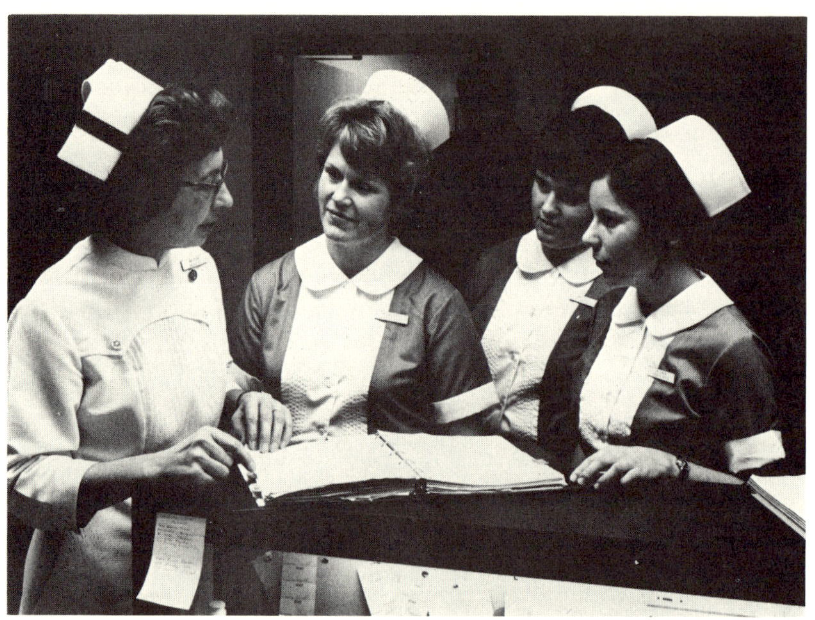

By the mid-1960s the school uniform had changed to a more practical style, and by the early 1970s the educational program reflected current nursing trends.

nursing facilitated the continuing advancement of nursing at Mary Hitchcock. Within seven years Mrs. Prouty had implemented this advanced type of nursing on nearly every major hospital service. The clinical specialists established teaching programs and offered consultation to nursing staffs as they helped to focus on the changing needs of patients and their families. In 1974 she, like Miss Straw before her, was obliged to direct the school of nursing for one year when another vacancy occurred in its administrative personnel.

Professional trends encouraged the development of the nursing staff of the hospital. The training and education department conducted educational programs and the clinical specialists worked with patients, families, and interdisciplinary team members as they emphasized the expanding nursing roles. Team nursing and later primary nursing enabled nurses to utilize the nursing process in a constructive manner and to promote changes when necessary. Methods of creative health care delivery and maintenance were constantly explored.

In 1978 William L. Wilson retired and James W. Varnum became the Executive Director of Mary Hitchcock Memorial Hospital. In 1979 Marilyn P. Prouty was appointed to the position of Administrator for Nursing.

The School Of Nursing

As the school adopted current educational trends the older task-oriented methods of teaching were replaced by more creative techniques. Instructors promoted good correlation of theory and clinical experiences and urged the students to use a problem-solving approach to nursing care. The broader educational base and an in-depth study of the nursing process resulted in an overall strengthening of students' nursing skills.

During these years of development and innovation the school experienced further change as several directors managed its affairs within a short period of time. They were: Katherine Schenk, 1960-1968; Marion McGrath, 1968-1970; Alice Straw, 1970-1971; Clair E. McGinley, 1971-1974; Marilyn P. Prouty,* 1974-1975; Hilda Batchelder, 1975-1980.

The long-standing problem of retaining qualified faculty members continued for the turnover rate was high. Some courses had new instructors every couple of years but this did not seem to affect the quality of education received by students.

Many persons seeking a career in nursing at this time selected a diploma program although baccalaureate schools were often recommended. Some prospective students relied on tradition in making the decision, others were influenced by guidance counselors, family, or friends.

Those who entered the Mary Hitchcock school of nursing chose it for a variety of reasons. Many recalled the warmth shown by school personnel at the admission interview, some liked the Hanover area, and nearly all were impressed by the hospital's clinical facilities. In addition the school was conducted on an academic year after 1971, and this appealed to most. (Some diploma schools were still in session all year.)

The school's curriculum was arranged to provide about half of the theoretical instruction in the first year. Students attended classes in biological, physical, and behavioral sciences as well as introductory

* Marilyn P. Prouty assigned duties of "administrative assistant" to Caroline Shearman, a non-nurse faculty member who had been at the school for some years. Miss Shearman conducted the school's day-to-day business under Mrs. Prouty's direction.

nursing. These courses established the base of knowledge essential to further study of nursing.*

Early clinical experiences were carefully planned and well supervised but they always provoked acute anxiety in most of the students. Often the first assignment was to simply talk with a patient for a specified period of time and many of the students were amazed at how difficult that was! They progressed to more complicated nursing mea-

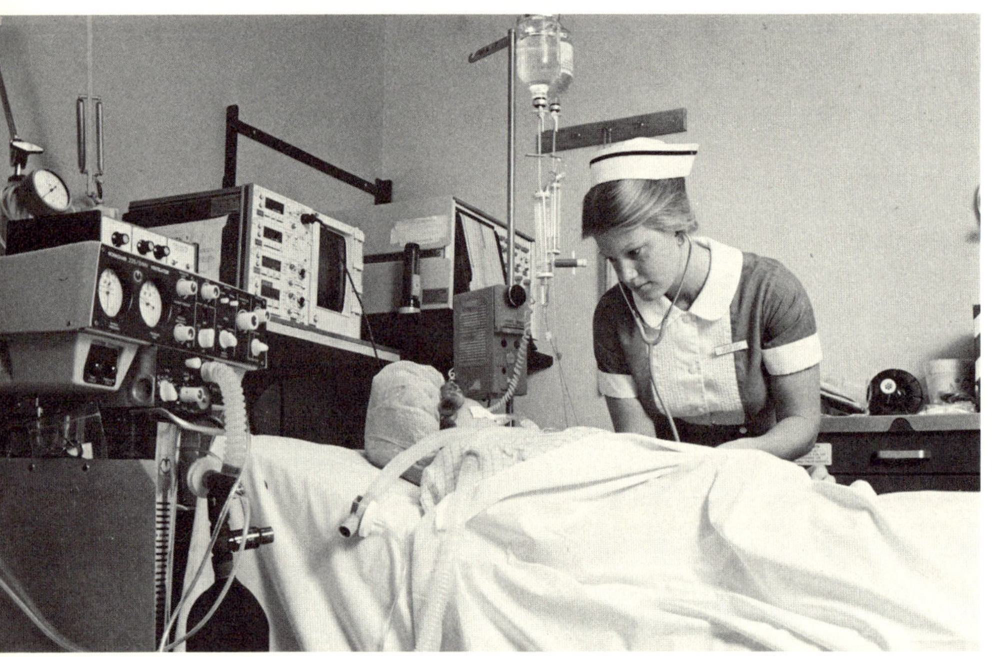

As students advanced in their training they encountered the challenge of complex nursing needs.

sures such as bedmaking, vital sign monitoring, and eventually the care of one patient. As the hospital environment became more familiar, those experiences produced less anxiety.

The second and third years offered different challenges for students as they cared for patients adjusting to altered life styles and complex health problems. They also had opportunities to observe nurses in nonhospital settings and they attended clinics, nursery schools, and other facilities. Instructors and students continually

* In 1976 and 1977 sociology and psychology courses were given by instructors from the University System of New Hampshire and provided eight credits.

evaluated the educational benefits of these experiences and sought to utilize them constructively.

Students were exposed to a variety of models of nursing care. They worked within the structures of team nursing, total patient care, and primary nursing. During the three years they also had opportunities to observe and work with the clinical specialist nurses in the hospital.

Clinical conferences helped assure correlation of learned theory to nursing situations and were held daily. Often students directed these sessions, presenting problems or ideas to the group. According to school philosophy, students progressed from simple to complex in all aspects of learning, and this concept was carried out in the clinical experiences also.

As Mary Hitchcock Hospital increased services and expanded its facilities it was no longer necessary to continue the affiliating programs. In 1963 the school discontinued its affiliation with the Boston Lying-In Hospital and the students returned to the obstetrical unit at Mary Hitchcock for maternity nursing. Although the unit was small the students were able to work there as well as in a variety of settings relating to that specialty. They cared for patients in the hospital unit and also rotated through the Hitchcock Clinic and other outpatient programs. When possible they were assigned to work with a family during the prenatal period, during delivery, and afterward. Most students enjoyed this type of experience. *

The pediatric nursing affiliation was eliminated in 1968 and again the students returned to Mary Hitchcock. This unit was also small but creative experiences were offered there and in several outpatient clinics and well-child programs. Students also learned about play therapy as they spent time with the "play lady" and the children hospitalized at Mary Hitchcock.

The Dartmouth-Hitchcock Mental Health Center was used for psychiatric/mental health nursing experiences in 1970. The community mental health center was vastly different from the state hospitals where previous groups of students had worked. Here the nurses obtained a slightly different view of mental illness as they worked with patients on a short term basis. Faculty arranged field trips and observational experiences at the state facilities so that the students could compare and contrast the different approaches to psychiatric nursing.

* A brief obstetrical rotation was arranged with the Alice Peck Day Hospital in Lebanon, New Hampshire, in 1972, and the Mary Hitchcock students received some experience in that hospital's maternity unit. This rotation was not continued however.

The first male student entered the Mary Hitchcock Memorial Hospital School of Nursing in 1965, and a total of eleven men graduated from the program during the next fifteen years. The school also began to admit "day" students and this allowed more men and women to pursue nursing education at the school. While some students preferred to live off campus for financial or other reasons, the majority of the day students were older men and women who had been out of school for some time, or who had family responsibilities. Their educational program was the same as that of the other students but since they did not live at the school they were usually less involved with student social activities.

In 1966 the positions of counselor and health director were combined and one person functioned in these capacities. For a time the school had a health office in the '50 Building and the health director/counselor attended to routine health needs of students. (Eventually this position was eliminated as student health services were expanded and counseling was offered by persons not directly connected with the school.) As the duties surrounding the maintenance of student records, applications for admission, and related items became more complex, the school added a registrar to its staff. A secretary had been employed at the school for several years and it soon became necessary to hire a clerk.

In 1969 the school completed a three-year project, assisted by a federal grant, which improved the library. This need had been apparent for some time and the library was relocated in a larger, well-designed space and a fully qualified librarian was hired. Library services were expanded and journal holdings and audio-visual teaching aides were increased. The new library served hospital personnel and others as well as the student nurses.

The school participated in recruitment programs at times and usually the registrar and students at the nursing school were involved in these activities. "Career days" were held at high schools throughout New England and representatives of Mary Hitchcock's nursing school attended these and other programs to present information about the school and answer questions. The nursing school also hosted open houses and interested persons could visit the school and learn about nursing education.

Students were active in academic affairs and elected representatives to serve on various school and hospital committees. Communications were good between the faculty and student groups and they worked together on many projects. Students were involved in assisting faculty on several revisions of the grading policy, and in later years they interviewed applicants for faculty positions. In 1976 a Student Bill of Rights was written and a grievance committee established. A judicial committee dealt with infractions of dormitory rules, and the self-governing system was used constructively.

Dormitory life changed drastically and quickly during these years as there was more emphasis placed on the responsibility for their own behavior. Students living there were subject to few restrictions and rules were directed toward the promotion of a safe, pleasant atmosphere in which to live.

After 1973 the school did not provide students' meals and many elected to prepare food in the limited kitchen facilities of the residences. It required the combined efforts of students, faculty, and administration to set guidelines for food preparation after a series of electrical "blackouts" had occurred at the school. The students worked out the problems and demonstrated their ability to compromise.

By 1974 parietal visiting privileges were established and the students no longer signed in and out of the dormitory. It was their responsibility to provide guidelines for activities in the residences and often students shared some of the duties of the proctor. The conventional role of housemothers had been replaced by proctors who functioned in similar capacities.

As more emphasis was placed on student needs the health service was moved to Dick Hall's House and the hospital contracted with the Dartmouth College Health Service for ambulatory and infirmary care. Students were encouraged to take responsibility for their own health care and to seek assistance when necessary.

The school helped those seeking financial aid by exploring possible sources of funding with them. The hospital maintained a loan fund (which the nursing school's alumnae association contributed to regularly) and a financial aid officer was available to work with students applying for loans, or state or federal funding.

Continued efforts had been made by faculty members to implement and review the school's curriculum while considering recommendations of the NLN. Consultants from that agency were hired to attend workshops and assist faculty in focusing on areas of concern. These occasions gave Mary Hitchcock instructors the opportunity to view the school in relation to the larger sphere of nursing education. The recommendations from the revisit in 1965 were analyzed and acted

Modern dormitory rooms enhanced life at the school as students pursued their academic, social, and personal interests.

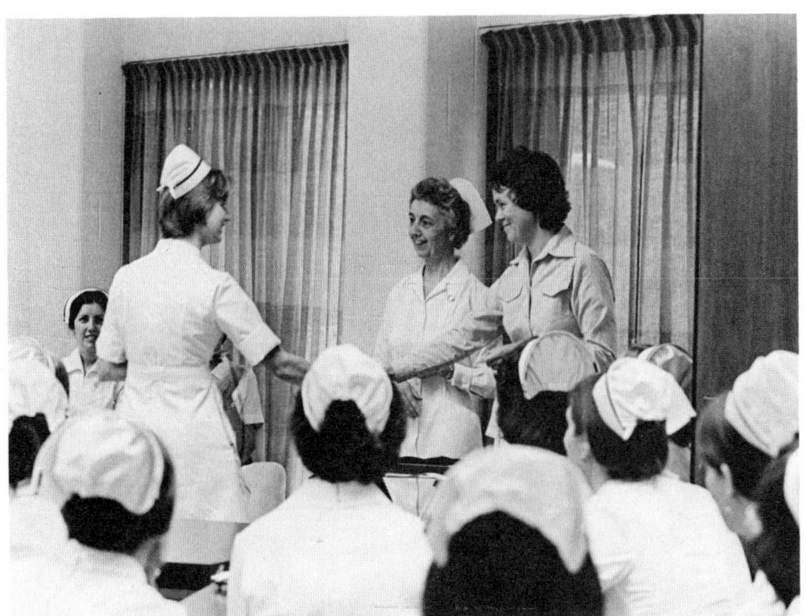

In recent years students received the school pin at a Senior / Faculty breakfast before graduation.

upon over a period of several years. In 1971 Miss Straw observed the attempts by students and faculty and said: ". . . They exert a continuous effort to enhance and strengthen our program."

The NLN visit of 1973, however, resulted in twenty-five recommendations which constituted a "warning" and necessitated a written progress report to be filed with the agency in 1974. The school had somehow fallen behind and there was much work to be done. With the aid of another consultant the faculty organization revised and restated objectives, rewrote policies, and devised a plan for the systematic evaluation of the school. Nearly every aspect of the school's operation was examined. Weekly meetings and work sessions were held and each faculty member assumed some responsibility in the effort. The group scrutinized each recommendation and carefully implemented action to meet the criteria. The progress report was submitted on schedule and was declared acceptable. The next accreditation visit was scheduled for 1978.

The school also sought continued state approval under the jurisdiction of the New Hampshire Board of Nursing Education and Nurse Registration. This agency also sent representatives to the school

Graduation 1977; for more than eighty years the school had graduated nurses well prepared to assume their new roles.

periodically and their evaluations and recommendations were often similar to those of the NLN. The faculty submitted reports and evidence of progress when requested and state approval was maintained.

Since accreditation or approval from these agencies was important to nursing education at Mary Hitchcock the school personnel accepted the suggestions and evaluations as constructive.

For several years there had been much discussion within many groups concerning nursing education at Mary Hitchcock. The School of Nursing Advisory Committee addressed the issue many times and faculty groups explored alternatives. Dialogue was conducted with colleges to consider using the clinical facilities for an academic program, and in March 1974 Marilyn P. Prouty led a conference to examine the future of nursing education at the Dartmouth-Hitchcock Medical Center. (This was the first major focus on the future of nursing education within the context of the medical center).

In 1976, at the direction of Marilyn P. Prouty and Hilda Batchelder, Martha Adams, who was then assistant director of the nursing school, undertook an exploratory project which echoed the findings of the

Over the last decade a full time librarian and expanded facilities provided comprehensive library services to both students and hospital staff.

statewide study by Chooporian and Craig as well as those of the major national studies. In view of the national trends in nursing education, the expanding facilities of the Dartmouth Hitchcock Medical Center, and the increasing need for specialized nursing there, she recommended that the Mary Hitchcock Memorial Hospital consider a decision to phase out its diploma program. A second proposal suggested the consideration of the facility as a clinical center for academic nursing education.

In 1977 the faculty organization voted to recommend to the Board of Trustees that the school of nursing be phased out. After consideration the board adopted that recommendation while indicating the hospital's commitment to nursing education. The authorization of a project director enabled the planning for the future of academic nursing education to begin.

The work of phasing out the school began immediately as each school alumna and prospective student received letters explaining the decision. The students at the school had opportunities to discuss their feelings on the matter and to ask questions. Administrative personnel and faculty members responded to the community's remarks and answered its questions. The course of events and the subsequent action taken was well summed up by Marilyn P. Prouty when she stated,

National trends which have developed as a result of a number of studies mandate that professional nurses be prepared in academic settings. Increasingly complex methods of delivering health care give support to the need for nurses to have a broader based preparation which can be provided only in an academic program.

Epilogue

UNDER THE experienced and skillful direction of Hilda Batchelder, the Mary Hitchcock Memorial Hospital School of Nursing began a well-planned procedure for phasing out its educational program. In the fall of 1977 the last class (to graduate in 1980) entered the school. As each faculty group promoted its final class to the next year, that level was phased out. Thus in 1978-79 there were two classes at the school and in 1979-80 only one.

During 1977 the faculty organization developed and adopted policies to govern the three-year period, insuring the maintenance of Mary Hitchcock's standards. As vacancies occurred in the faculty, attempts were made to fill the positions with qualified nursing school instructors whose jobs had already been terminated. In addition the Nursing Service Department and the Personnel Department of the hospital were supportive in offering assistance to those interested in working at Mary Hitchcock upon completion of faculty duties. An ad hoc committee helped members explore policies concerning faculty employment in the hospital and offered peer support. The faculty organization functioned with its various committees until 1979-80 when it became a committee of the whole.

Specific plans were implemented to provide the students with optimum services (health care, housing, etc.) and individual educational needs. Certain courses could not be repeated in the case of student failure or illness as the levels were phased out and the faculty prepared guidelines for dealing with that possible situation.

No major curriculum changes were undertaken and clinical experiences were still carefully planned. Some of the hospital units which had seemed to be overflowing with student nurses now offered

During the school's final year, students and faculty worked closely together to maintain standards.

a large choice of assignments, and care was given to choose those best suited to meet the educational objectives of the particular course. New material was incorporated as courses were updated and instructors attended workshops and conferences to keep abreast of developments within nursing. The school made significant progress in teaching the nursing process and its implementation in the clinical setting. Both students and faculty maintained a high level of educational interest and motivation.

The academic year of 1977-78 began as usual but the finality of the schools's closure emerged with emotional overtones as the year progressed. Faculty and students alike sought opportunities to talk about those feelings and find constructive outlets for them. Some organized discussion groups and meetings were effective. Simultaneously both faculty and students carried on with the work of nursing education, though for some that first year of the phasing out might have been the most difficult.

In 1978-79, with two classes remaining, the utilization of the school's physical plant for other purposes began. Students' rooms and faculty offices were moved into the '37 and '50 Buildings as Medical

Center departments were moved into Billings-Lee. The following year the school occupied the '50 Building while arrangements were made for occupation of the '37 Building. The school maintained the living room of Billings-Lee which served as an entrance to the school, and a reception area for visitors. It also provided a place for the proctor's desk, mail distribution, and student gatherings.

In the fall of 1978 the school was visited by representatives from the NLN for accreditation purposes. With only twelve recommendations the school was granted full accreditation until its closure. Miss Batchelder wrote, "It assures the graduates that criteria for a quality program which have been accepted by the profession are being met and that graduates who wish to pursue further education have met this requirement for admission." The faculty had taken action on most of the recommendations by the end of the year. The school had the option of submitting a closing report to the NLN in lieu of a visitation, but Miss Batchelder and the faculty members sought to conduct the school with the highest standards possible until its closing and it was felt that the NLN visitation would be constructive.

In 1979-80 only one class of senior students, a faculty of six, the director, and a small staff comprised the school of nursing. The size of the group brought about a closeness (similar to older days) as well as efforts for superior achievement. A strong feeling of merit and accomplishment prevailed.

The faculty assisted the students with the work of student government and other student committees in reorganizing them into a committee of the whole. Students were very involved in school affairs as well as the plans surrounding the program's closure. Those serving on various committees worked effectively with others and accepted tasks of responsibility.

In the fall of 1979 the school hosted the final visit of the New Hampshire State Board of Nursing Education and Nurse Registration. This added assurance that state requirements were being met, and it also served as a formal concluding visit.

During that final year those at the school and persons connected with it began to feel an increased sense of loyalty and pride as well as a growing anticipation for the future. This diploma school had come full cycle and it was now time for it to take its rightful place in nursing history.

For eighty-seven years the Mary Hitchcock Memorial Hospital School of Nursing had pursued excellence in nursing education and had rendered faithful service to the hospital and the community. Now its purpose was accomplished and Hiram Hitchcock's legacy had been fulfilled.

Careful planning and close cooperation by medical center and nursing school staff ensured a smooth transition to the future.

Appendices

CURRICULUM

The Mary Hitchcock Memorial Hospital
Training School for Nurses

Circa 1905

Length of Program: two years
Vacation: six weeks

THEORY

Subjects:	Hours of class or lecture given by physician	nurse	Clinical demonstration or laboratory hours
Principles & Practice of nursing		60	
Sanitation and hygiene	4		
General care and observation of patients	4		
Physiology of circulation and respiration	4		
Anatomy	6		
Obstetrics	8		
Sepsis, Asepsis, Antisepsis	2		
Before and after Abdominal Surgery	2		
Preparation for Operation in private homes	2		
Food Principles and Cooking	8		12
Contagious diseases	4		
Medical diseases	4		
Bacteriology	4		
Disinfection	2		
Analysis of Urine	4		
Bandaging and Splints	2		
Materia Medica	4		
Diseases of Eye and Ear	4		
Emergencies	2		
Ethics of Nursing	2		
Massage			12

NURSING PRACTICE

Area of Practice	Weeks	Hours*
Hospital wards, (integrating all services)	98	6,272
Home nursing	10	1,400
Operating Room	17	1,020

* Hours computed on an average of student records. The actual time in different areas varied with each student.

Curriculum Circa 1928

Theoretical Content	Hours	Instruction By
Practical Nursing	120	Nursing personnel
Medical Nursing	32	Nursing personnel and physician
Surgical Nursing	32	Nursing personnel and physician
Obstetrical Nursing	20	Nursing personnel and physician
Pediatrics	30	Nursing personnel and physician
Communicable diseases	15	Nursing personnel and physician
Bacteriology & Hygiene	20	Nursing personnel and physician
Anatomy & Physiology	80	Nursing personnel
Materia Medica	32	Nursing personnel
Mental diseases	15	Nursing personnel and professor
Ethics & History of nursing	16	Nursing personnel
Dietetics	26	Dietician
Massage	12	Nursing personnel
Eye, ear, nose & throat diseases	8	Physician
First Aid	4	Physician
Sanitation & personal hygiene	6	Nursing personnel
Drugs and solutions	12	Nursing personnel
Bandaging	8	Nursing personnel and physician
Pathology	10	Physician
Operating room technique	5	Nursing personnel
Laboratory Technique	4	Nursing personnel
Professional problems	15	Nursing personnel

In 1931 advanced nursing, General review, and Chemistry were added to the curriculum and those subjects were taught by nursing personnel.

Practical Experience	Weeks
Medical service	32
Surgical service	32
Obstetrics	12
Operating room	12
Pediatrics	12
Dietetics	4 to 6

The above information was obtained from Mary Hitchcock Memorial Hospital School of Nursing records on file at the New Hampshire Board of Nursing Education and Nurse Registration, Concord, New Hampshire.

LENGTH OF PROGRAM: 3 years
PROBATIONARY PERIOD: 4 months

Curriculum Circa 1945

Theoretical Content	Hours	Instruction By
Practical nursing	190	Nursing personnel
Medical nursing	45	Nursing personnel and physician
Surgical nursing	40	Nursing personnel and physician
Obstetrical nursing	40	Nursing personnel and physician
Pediatrics	36	Nursing personnel and physician
Communicable diseases	21	Nursing personnel and physician
Bacteriology	45	Nursing personnel and physician
Anatomy & Physiology	110	Nursing personnel
Materia Medica	35	Nursing personnel
Psychiatry & psychology	10	Physician
Ethics and history of nursing	35	Nursing personnel
Dietetics and nutrition	30	Dietician
Massage	5	Physical therapist
Eye, ear, nose & throat diseases	16	Nursing personnel and physician
First Aid	22	Physician
Personal hygiene	20	Nursing personnel
Drugs and solutions	25	Nursing personnel
Orthopedics	10	Nursing personnel and physician
Pathology	28	Physician
Operating room technique	16	Nursing personnel
Urology	5	Nursing personnel and physician
Professional Problems	30	Nursing personnel
Diet therapy	30	Nursing personnel and physician
Gynecological nursing	15	Nursing personnel and physician
Advanced nursing	24	Nursing personnel
Chemistry	30	Nursing personnel
Public sanitation & community hygiene	18	Nursing personnel and professor
Study habits	5	Nursing personnel

Practical Experience	Weeks
Medical Service	20-32
Surgical Service	20-32
Obstetrics	12
Operating room	8
Pediatrics	12
Dietetics	6
Psychiatric service	12*

* The theoretical and practical experience in psychiatric nursing were an affiliated course at the New Hampshire Hospital, Concord, New Hampshire.

LENGTH OF PROGRAM: 3 years
PROBATIONARY PERIOD: 4-5 months

Curriculum / 1960

Semester	Course Title	Total Hours of Instruction	Planned Classroom Instruction and Laboratory Hours	Planned Clinical Conference Hours	Planned Clinical Laboratory Hours or Weeks
30 wks.	First Aid	26	26	0	0
	Integrated Science	240	240	0	0
	Nursing I	180	180	0	3 wks.
	Nutrition I	30	30	0	0
	Human Relations I	40	40	0	0
	Human Relations II	40	40	0	0
	Professional Adjustments I	30	30	0	0
	History of Nursing	15	15	0	0
18 wks.	Nutrition II (Communications)	30	30	0	0
	Human Relations III	15	15	0	0
	Pharmacology II	60	60	0	0
	Medical-Surgical Nursing I	193	161	32	18 wks.
24 wks.	Nursing in the Operating Room	50	40	10	8 wks.
	Diet Therapy Experience	8	0	8	4 wks
	Medical-Surgical Nursing II	24	0	24	12 wks.
24 wks.	Obstetrical Nursing	84	60	26	12 wks.
	Nursing of Children	90	65	25	12 wks.
12 wks.	Psychiatric Nursing	170	130	40	12 wks.
38 wks.	Medical-Surgical Nursing III	69	34	35	38 wks.
	Professional Adjustments II	30	30	0	0
	Senior Seminar	8	8	0	0

Organization Plan of the Curriculum / 1977

Yr.	Tri-mester	Wks.	Course	Class Units	Class Hrs.	Laboratory Units	Laboratory Hrs.	Total Units	Total Hrs.
1	1	12	Introductory Nursing 100	7	84	2	48	9	132
			Correlated Physical and Biological Sciences 110	6	72	1	24	7	96
			Totals	13	156	3	72	16	228
1	2	12	Introductory Nursing 101	7	84	2	49	9	132
			Correlated Physical and Biological Sciences III	6	72	1	24	7	96
			Introductory Sociology	4 cr.	48			4	48
			Totals	17	204	3	72	20	276
1	3	12	Introductory Nursing 102	7	84	2.5	60	9.5	144
			Correlated Physical and Biological Sciences 112	6	72	1	24	7	96
			Introductory Psychology	4 cr.	48			4	48
			Totals	17	204	3.5	84	20.5	288
2	1	12	Intermediate Medical/Surgical Nursing 201	6	72	11	264	17	336
2	2	12	Nursing of Children 202	8	96	9	216	17	312
2	3	12	Maternal/Newborn Nursing 203	8	103	9	200	17	303
			Totals	22	271	29	680	51	951
3	1	12	Nursing Leadership 301	8	96	9	232	17	328
3	2	12	Advanced Medical/Surgical Nursing 302	8	100	9	219	17	319
3	3	12	Psychiatric/Mental Health Nursing 303	7.8	93	8.2	198	16	291
			Totals	23.8	289	26.2	649	50	938

BIBLIOGRAPHY

Adams, Martha, "A Report to the University of New Hampshire School of Health Studies, Department of Nursing, and Mary Hitchcock Memorial Hospital School of Nursing." "Exploratory Project to Determine Feasibility of Extension of the University of New Hampshire School of Health Studies Department of Nursing Clinical Facilities to Include Mary Hitchcock Memorial Hospital, and The Future of Mary Hitchcock Memorial Hospital School of Nursing." April through June, 1976.

Amsden, John P., *The Mary Hitchcock Memorial Hospital Its Third Quarter Century.* Hanover, New Hampshire, 1968.

"ANA's First Position On Education for Nursing." *American Journal of Nursing,* December, 1965, pp. 106-11.

ANA Platform, 1960-1962. *American Journal of Nursing,* August 1960, p. 1100.

Annual Reports of the Mary Hitchcock Memorial Hospital School of Nursing to the New Hampshire Board of Nursing Education and Nurse Registration. 1911-1978.

Beattie, Edith M., "Nurse Draft Legislation and the American Nurses' Association—A Summary." *American Journal of Nursing,* July, 1945, pp. 546-8.

Brown, Esther Lucile, *Nursing for the Future.* New York, the Russell Sage Foundation, 1948.

Bullough, Bonnie, and Bullough, Vern L., *The Emergence of Modern Nursing.* New York, The Macmillan Company, 1964.

Burgess, May Ayres, "Problems Involved in the Grading Program." *American Journal of Nursing,* December, 1926, pp. 919-27.

__________, "Six Questions of Grading." *American Journal of Nursing,* January, 1928, pp. 25-6.

__________, "Where Does Nursing Want to Go?" *American Journal of Nursing,* May, 1928 pp. 481-5.

__________, *Nurses, Patients* and *Pocketbooks.* New York, National League of Nursing Education, 1928.

__________, "What the Cost Study Showed." *American Journal of Nursing,* May, 1932, pp. 427-32.

__________, *Nursing Schools Today and Tomorrow.* New York, National League of Nursing Education, 1934.

Ciske, Karen L., "Accountability—The Essence of Primary Nursing." *American Journal of Nursing,* May, 1979, pp. 890-94.

Chooporian, Teresa, and Craig, Margaret, "Statewide Interdisciplinary Planning Project for Nursing and Nursing Education," "Future Directions for Nursing in New Hampshire." Report of First Year Project Activities and Recommendations, November, 1975.

Cohn, Isidore, "A Plea for Bedside Nurse Training" (Ed). *American Journal of Surgery,* February, 1951, pp. 147-50.

Committee on Nursing and Nursing Education in the United States, *Nursing and Nursing Education in the United States.* New York, The Macmillan Company, 1928.

Davis, Mary E. P., "Organization, Or Why Belong?" *American Journal of Nursing,* March, 1912, pp. 474-7.

Davis, Michael M., "Public Responsibility for The Education of Nurses." *American Journal of Nursing,* July, 1933, pp. 694-700.

Densford, Katherine J., "ANA Testimony on Proposed Draft Legislation." *American Journal of Nursing,* May, 1945, pp. 383-5.

Dock, Lavinia L., *A Short History of Nursing From the Earliest Times to the Present Day.* New York, Putnam, 1920.

Dolan, Josephine A., *History of Nursing,* 12th Edition. Philadelphia. W. B. Saunders Company, 1968.

__________, *Nursing In Society.* Philadelphia, W. B. Saunders Company, 1978.

Faddis, Margene C., *A Nursing School Comes of Age.* Cleveland, The Alumni Association of the Frances Payne Bolton School of Nursing, 1973.

Flanagan, Lydia, *One Strong Voice; the Story of the American Nurses' Association.* Kansas City, American Nurses' Association, 1976.

Goldmark, Josephine C., "Nursing and Nursing Education in The United States." Report of the Committee for the Study of Nursing Education and a Report of a Survey by Josephine Goldmark. New York, Macmillan Company, 1923.

Goodnow, Minnie, *Nursing History* 7th Edition. Philadelphia, W. B. Saunders Company, 1944.

Goodrich, Annie W., (Report of Committee on Review of Constitution and By-Laws, American Society of Superintendents of Training Schools for Nurses.) *American Journal of Nursing,* June, 1905, pp. 618-21.

Griffin, Gerald Joseph, and Griffin, Joanne King, *History and Trends of Professional Nursing.* Saint Louis, C. V. Mosby Company, 1973.

Grow, Eugene Julius, "The Mary Hitchcock Memorial Hospital," *The Granite Monthly,* November, 1896, pp. 247-58.

Hampton, Isabel A., et al., *Nursing of The Sick–1893.* New York, McGraw Hill Book Company, Inc., 1949.

The Hanover Gazette, Nov. 26, 1892, May 6, 1893, June 3, 1893, Hanover, N.H.

Hilliard, Amy M., "Factors for Consideration in the Improvement of Our Schools of Nursing." *American Journal of Nursing,* August, 1920, pp. 910-12.

_________, "The Student Nurse," *American Journal of Nursing,* December, 1920, pp. 176-8.

Jamieson, Elizabeth M., Sewall, Mary F., and Gjertson, Lucille S., *Trends In Nursing History, Their Social, International and Ethical Relationships.* 5th Edition. W. B. Saunders Co., Philadelphia, 1959.

Jamme, Anna C., "The California Eight-Hour Law for Women." *American Journal of Nursing,* April, 1919, pp. 525-30.

Kalisch, Philip A., and Kalisch, Beatrice J., *The Advance of American Nursing.* Little, Brown and Company. Boston, 1978.

Logan, Laura, "The National League of Nursing Education." *School and Society,* July 1923, pp. 51-2.

Lord, John King, *The Mary Hitchcock Memorial Hospital, Its First Quarter Century.* The Trustees, Hanover, N.H., 1919.

Manthey, Marie, "Primary Nursing Is Alive and Well in The Hospital." *American Journal of Nursing,* January, 1973, pp. 83-87.

Mary Hitchcock Memorial Hospital, *Annual Report,* 1893-1947. Hanover, N.H. Concord, N.H.

Mary Hitchcock Memorial Hospital, *Annual Review,* 1947-1951. Hanover, N.H.

Mary Hitchcock Memorial Hospital, *A New Era of Service.* Hanover, N.H., 1952.

Mary Hitchcock Memorial Hospital, *Annual Review,* 1953-1979. Hanover, N.H.

Mary Hitchcock Memorial Hospital Alumnae Association, Treasurer's Book. 1910-1919.

Mary Hitchcock Memorial Hospital, *Hitchcock Highlights,* selected monthly volumes, 1953-1979.

Mary Hitchcock Memorial Hospital School of Nursing, "Follow-Up Study of Mary Hitchcock Memorial Hospital School of Nursing Graduates In the Classes of 1974, 1975, 1976." February, 1978.

Mary Hitchcock Memorial Hospital School of Nursing, *Self Evaluation Report.* 1974 and 1978.

McManus, R. Louise, "What Colleges and Universities Offer the Practicing Nurse." *American Journal of Nursing.* December, 1954, pp. 1478-80.

Mereness, Dorothy A., and Taylor, Cecelia Monat, *Essentials of Psychiatric Nursing.* 9th Ed. The C. V. Mosby Co. Saint Louis, 1974.

Modern Hospital: "Smith College (Northampton Mass.) Aids Nursing Education at Cooley Hospital." October, 1950, p. 172.

Montag, Mildred L., "Technical Education In Nursing." *American Journal of Nursing,* May, 1963, pp. 100-3.

Morison, Samuel Eliot, *The Oxford History of the American People.* New York, Oxford University Press, 1965.

Nahm, Helen, "Temporary Accreditation." *American Journal of Nursing,* August, 1952, pp. 997-1001.

_________, "Continuity and Progression in Nursing Education." *American Journal of Nursing,* June, 1958, pp. 845-7.

National Commission for The Study of Nursing and Nursing Education, Summary Report and Recommendations. *American Journal of Nursing,* February, 1970, pp. 279-94.

National League for Nursing, "Division of Nursing Education: Educational Resources for the Preparation of Nurses." *Nursing Outlook,* January, 1958, pp. 33-8.

National League for Nursing, *Nursing Data Book.* New York, National League for Nursing, 1978.

New Hampshire Board of Nursing Education and Nurse Registration. Summary of Legislation of Nursing in New Hampshire.

New Hampshire State Commission on Nursing. *Report on the Various Phases of Nursing,* November, 1954.

New Hampshire State Nurses Association, *Fiftieth Anniversary, 1906-1956.* Compiled by Mary T. Madden, and Marilyn Sorrenty, assisted by the New Hampshire Student Nurse Association.

Nutting, M. Adelaide, "Thirty Years of Progress In Nursing." *American Journal of Nursing,* September, 1923, pp. 1027-35.

Palmer, Sophia F., "The Effect of State Registration Upon Training Schools." *American Journal of Nursing,* July, 1905, pp. 656-666.

————, The Essential Features of a Bill for the State Registration of Nurses and How to Pass it." *American Journal of Nursing,* March, 1907, pp. 428-33.

Petry, Lucile, "U.S. Cadet Corps Established Under the Bolton Act." *American Journal of Nursing,* August, 1943, pp. 704-8.

————, "Making The Most of the Senior Cadet Period." *American Journal of Nursing,* June, 1944, pp. 572-4.

————, "The U.S. Cadet Corps—A Summing Up." *American Journal of Nursing,* December, 1945, pp. 1027-8.

Perkins, Sylvia, *A Centennial Review, 1878-1973, of the Massachusetts General Hospital School of Nursing.* School of Nursing Nurses' Alumnae Association, Stinehour Press, 1975.

Pfefferkorn, Blanche, "Adjustments in the Educational Program for Nursing." *American Journal of Nursing,* November, 1924, pp. 1126-32.

Prouty, Marilyn P., and Batchelder, Hilda, "Information on Nursing and Nursing Needs at the Dartmouth-Hitchcock Medical Center." 1977.

Richards, Linda, "Early Days In The First American Training Schools For Nurses." *American Journal of Nursing,* December, 1915, pp. 174-9.

————, "Thirty Years of Progress." *American Journal of Nursing,* January, 1904, pp. 263-7.

Richardson, Leon B., *A History of the Mary Hitchcock Memorial Hospital Fifty Years of Service,* 1893-1943. Hanover, N.H., 1943.

Robb, Isabel Hampton, "The Affiliation of Training Schools for Nurses for Educational Purposes." *American Journal of Nursing,* July, 1905, pp. 666-79.

Roberts, J., and Thetis, M. G., "The Women's Movement and Nursing." *Nursing Forum,* Volume XII, No. 3, 1973.

Roberts, Mary M., *American Nursing History and Interpretation.* New York, the Macmillan Co., 1954.

"Rockefeller Foundation and Nursing Education." *American Journal of Nursing,* April, 1920, p. 525.

Rowland, Howard S., *The Nurses Almanac.* Germantown, Md., Aspen Systems Corporation, 1978.

Safier, Gwendolyn, *Contemporary American Leaders in Nursing: An Oral History.* New York, McGraw Hill, 1977.

Sanner, Margaret C., *Trends and Professional Adjustments in Nursing.* Philadelphia, Saunders, 1962.

The ANA: Can a Professional Association Be a Trade Union Too?" *Hospitals,* September, 1974, p. 103.

"Too Many Nurses in These Localities." *American Journal of Nursing,* March, 1930, p. 344, March 1932, p. 329, April 1932, p. 467.

Woodward, Ellen S., "The WPA and Nursing." *American Journal of Nursing,* September, 1937, pp. 994-7.

In addition many miscellaneous documents, papers, and records of the Mary Hitchcock Memorial Hospital School of Nursing, as well as school bulletins, and handbooks were used in the compilation of data.

Representations of student life were obtained from anonymous responses to surveys of seven hundred graduates of the school and actual interviews with more than thirty persons. Every attempt has been made to present factual information.

When discrepancies were found in historical information, the author used material on file at the New Hampshire Board of Nursing Education and Nurse Registration, Concord, N.H., as the official source and those facts appear in the text.

ALUMNAE ASSOCIATION*

Charter Members, May 31, 1910

Ada Morey Goss / 1898
Harriet Spaulding Muzzy / 1898
Sara Corning / 1899
Edith Samuel / 1900
Lucia Shattuck Gray / 1904
Lillian L. Knox / 1906
Bertha M. Hopkins / 1907
Emma L. Foster / 1907
Jeannie McLeod / 1908
Mary E. Jordan / 1909
Louise M. Schmidt / 1906
Harriet W. Horton / 1905
Bertha L. Walker / 1907
Laura M. Metcalf / 1906
Christie W. Robbins / 1905

Officers, December, 1979

Marion Simonds Fitzgerald 1933 President
Nellie Sweet Williams 1934 Secretary
Dora Jane Sargent Johnson 1929 Treasurer

* Recently the name of the association was officially changed to The Mary Hitchcock Memorial Hospital School of Nursing Alumnae Association. Today the group numbers nearly four hundred active members.

List of Illustrations

The illustrations in *Hiram Hitchcock's Legacy* were selected from more than five hundred photographs in personal collections, the files of the hospital and school of nursing, and the Dartmouth College Library. The author is deeply indebted to all who shared their personal photographs as well as to those who helped so much in the search for suitable illustrative material.

The photographs finally selected for inclusion, which are listed below in the order in which they appear in the volume, are from the files of the Mary Hitchcock Memorial Hospital School of Nursing; the Information Services Department of the Mary Hitchcock Memorial Hospital; the archives of Special Collections in the Dartmouth College Library; and the private collection of Faun Barney (MHMH 1923), Judith Chabot Churchard (MHMH 1967), Dora Jane Sargent Johnson (MHMH 1929), and Marion Stark Taylor (MHMH 1918).

Photographs by Jonathan Sa'adah, who was specially commissioned to record the activities of the nursing school during its final year of operation, appear on pages 118, 122, 125, 128, and 130.

Hiram Hitchcock v
Interior of hospital, 1893 8
Hospital porch 10
Rotunda and staircase 12
Private room, 1893 13
Superintendent's office, 1893 15
The East Ward 18
Official uniform, circa 1900 20
Students and staff, 1903 21
Students, 1910 23
Operating room 25
Student nurses, 1912 26
Alumnae group, early 1900s 30
Taking a break, about 1918 34
Off duty, about 1918 35
Liberty Bond parade, 1918 36
Pike House 43
Billings-Lee, 1921 46
Student room in Billings-Lee 47
Classroom, Billings-Lee, 1928 49
Reference Library, Billings-Lee, 1928 50
Hospital stairwell 54

Hospital dining room, 1920s 55
Classroom, Billings-Lee, 1920s 56
Part of student body, 1928 59
Superintendent and potential nurses, 1932 67
Nursing school addition under construction, 1937 72
Hospital scene, early 1940s 81
School basketball team, 1944 85
First year students, 1952 98
One-on-one instruction, 1950s 101
Memorial Day parade, 1952 104
School chorus, 1951 106
Dormitory living, 1960s 109
Main entrance of the hospital, 1970s 113
Informal instruction, 1970s 116
Nursing complexities of the 1970s 118
Modern dormitory room of the 1970s 122
School pin presentation 123
Graduation, 1977 124
Library conference, late 1970s 125
Student/faculty cooperation, final year 128
Planning for the future, 1979 130

INDEX

Accreditation, 92, 100, 103, 123, 124, 129
Adams, Martha, 124, 125
Administrator, Mary Hitchcock Memorial Hospital, 78, 95, 117
Administrator, nursing, 117, 130 illus.
Admission policies, 9, 11, 32, 82, 48, 98, 99, 120
Affiliations, 81, 82, 101, 103, 106, 107, 119
Air Force Nurse Corps, 92
Alice Peck Day Hospital, 119
Allen, Professor Chauncy C., 49
Allen, Professor Chauncy N., 66
Alumnae Association, 31, 37, 50, 51, 141
American Hospital Association, 77
American Journal of Nursing, 28, 61, 92
American Medical Association, 77
American Nurses' Association, 28, 29, 42, 61, 92, 94, 95, 113, 114
  Certification Program, 114
  Committee on Education, 94
  Position Paper on Education for Nursing, 94, 103
  Nurses for Political Action, 114
  American Red Cross, 76, 79
  American Revolution, 1
American Society of Superintendents of Training Schools, 28
Ancillary nursing personnel, 78, 79, 95, 96, 100
Army Nurse Corps, 33, 76
Assistant Administrator for nursing, 115, 116, 124, 126
Associate degree programs in nursing, 93
Auxiliary, Mary Hitchcock Memorial Hospital, 62, 63, 63 fn., 66, 79, 97
A Ward, 19, 69, 96

Baker Library, 111
Basketball team, Mary Hitchcock Memorial Hospital School of Nursing, 85 illus.
Bartlett, Edwin J., 43
Bartlett, Dr. Percy, 14
Batchelder, Hilda, 117, 124, 127, 129
"Big Sister" program, 84
Billings family, 22, 22 fn.
Billings, Frederick, 22, 22 fn.
Billings-Lee Home for Nurses, 22, 38, 46, 46 illus., 47, 49, 52, 53, 66, 67 illus., 71, 73, 80, 110, 111, 128, 129
Bolton, Frances Payne, 76
Boston Children's Hospital, 101, 103, 107
Boston City Hospital Training School, 15
Boston Lying-In Hospital, 101, 103, 107, 119
Boyle, Ellen, 49
Brattleboro Retreat, 49
Brown, Ester Lucile, 77
Bryant, Hazel, 45, 47, 49
'37 Building, Mary Hitchcock Memorial Hospital School of Nursing, 66, 72, illus., 73, 80, 86, 128, 129
'50 Building, Mary Hitchcock Memorial Hospital School of Nursing, 80, 107, 97, 111, 120, 128, 129
B Ward, 19, 96

California Nurses Association, 114
Callahan, Harold A., 78
Campion, James W. Jr., 78
Candy Stripers, 97
Carter X-ray Building, 62
Catalogue, Mary Hitchcock Memorial Hospital School of Nursing, 50, 97
Census, Mary Hitchcock Memorial Hospital School of Nursing, 65, 99
Chapel services, 53, 54, 109
Chicago World's Fair, 1893, 3, 28
Chopoorian, Teresa, 115, 125
Civil Defense, 97
Civil War, 2
Civil Works Administration, 61
Clinical Instruction, 11, 14, 23, 49, 53, 69, 70, 71, 80, 81, 105, 116, 118, illus., 119, 128, 128 illus.
Clinical specialists, 115, 116
Collective bargaining, 114
Collegiate preparation for nurses, 17, 92, 93, 102, 114, 115, 117, 124, 125, 126
Committee on the Grading of Nurses, 42
Committee on the Grading of Nursing Schools, 50, 64, 65
Committee for the Study of Nursing and Nursing Education in the United States, 38 fn., 42
Commissioner of Education, New Hampshire, 29
Communicable Disease Nursing, 67

Coolidge, Calvin, 60
Corning, Sara, 141
Craig, Margaret, 115, 125
Crosby, Dr. Dixi, 8
Council of National Defense, 36
Curriculum, 11, 14, 15, 22, 32, 35, 36, 48-49, 57, 58, 62, 64, 65, 68, 70, 81, 82, 94, 100, 101, 102, 107, 108, 117, 121, 127, 133-38
Curriculum Guide, National League of Nursing Education, 61, 62, 68

Dartmouth College, 22, 26, 43, 44, 49, 58, 59, 62, 66, 73, 86, 97, 107, 110, 111
Dartmouth College, health service, 121
Dartmouth Hitchcock Medical Center, 113 illus., 115, 124, 125, 128, 129
Dartmouth Hitchcock Mental Health Center, 115, 119
Dartmouth Medical School, 9, 59, 73, 86
Day students, Mary Hitchcock Memorial Hospital School of Nursing, 120
Depression, 45, 60, 61, 62, 63, 64, 66, 67, 70, 74
Dick Hall's House, 44, 62, 95, 121
Diet kitchen, 57, 58, 107
Director, Nursing Education, 96, 97, 99, 100, 102, 105
Director, Nursing Service, 96, 99, 100, 102, 105, 115, 123
Director, School of Nursing, 117, 123, 123 illus., 124, 127, 128, 130 illus.
Donation Day, 19, 34, 37, 44
Dowler, Marie V., 78, 82, 85, 86, 96
Danvers State Hospital, 103, 107

East Ward, 18 illus., 62, 64, 69
Educational Director, School of Nursing, 99
Edward C. Daniels Fund, 51 fn.
Enrollment, School of Nursing, 11, 36, 38, 65, 80, 97
Ernest N. Seavy Fund, 51 fn.
Exchange program, 22, 26 illus.
Executive Director, Mary Hitchcock Memorial Hospital, 117
Eye Clinic, 62

Faculty, 11, 14, 21 illus., 23 illus., 32, 36 illus., 49, 49 illus., 50, 56 illus., 64, 73, 80, 81, 85 illus., 99, 100, 101, 101 illus., 107, 116 illus., 117, 123 illus., 125, 126, 127, 128 illus., 129, 130 illus.
Faulkner Building, 95, 96, 99, 100, 104, 115
Faulkner, Mrs. Edward D., (Marianne), 79, 96
Federal Emergency Relief Fund, 61
Fernald, Mary Louise, 96, 100, 102, 105
Financial aid for students, 121
Fitch, Florence, 30
Fitzgerald, Marion Simonds, 141
Foster, Emma L., 141
Fraternities, Dartmouth College, 58, 73, 86
Freeman, John, 22 fn.
"French Flat," 52
Frost, Dr. Gilman D., 14

Gile, Dr. J. M., 14
Glee Club, 111
Glenn, Jessie, 15
Goal Three, 94
Goldmark Report, 42
Goss, Ada Morey, 141
Graduate Nurses of New Hampshire, 29, 31
Graduate nurses' registry, Mary Hitchcock Memorial Hospital, 63
Graduation, 15, 22, 23, 36, 124 illus.
Grey, Lucia Shattuck, 31, 141
Griffin, Rose E., 45, 49, 50, 51, 64, 65, 68, 69, 71, 74, 78
Guidance Counselor, 101, 120

Hall, Mr. and Mrs. Edward K., 44
Hall, Richard Drew, 44
Hamilton, James A., 45, 63, 65, 68
Hamington, Maude, 9
Hanover High School, 110
Head nurses, 9, 11, 12, 21 illus., 23, 23 illus., 24, 47, 55, 67, 99
Health Director, 99, 105, 120
Herbut, Helen, 115
Hill, Irja, 96, 102, 105, 115
Hitchcock Clinic, 45, 62, 81, 95, 119

Hitchcock, Dawn L., 19
Hitchcock, Hiram, 7, 8, 17, 18, 130
Hitchcock, Mary, 7, 8
Hitler, Adolph, 75
Home nursing, 13, 14, 26
Honor system, 110
"Hoovervilles," 60
Hopkins, Bertha M., 141
Horton, Harriet W., 45, 47, 48, 141
Hospital Aid Committee, 44
Housemothers, 86, 111, 121
House staff, 21 illus., 35
Howe Library, 111

Industrial Revolution, 2

Johnson, Dora Jane Sargent, 141
Jordan, Mary E., 141

Knapp, Dr. Henry Lee, 35
Knox, Lillian L., 141
Korean War, 92

Ladies Auxiliary, Boston Children's Hospital, 107
Lane, Susan K., 30
Leach, Theresa G., 9, 15
Lee family, 22, 22 fn.
Legislation for nursing, 16, 93, 95
Lend-Lease Act, 75
Liberty Bond Parade, 36 illus., 37 fn.
Librarian, school of nursing, 120, 125 illus.
Library, school of nursing, 50, 80, 97, 120, 125 illus.
Lillian Louise Knox Fund, 51 fn.
Lockerby, Anna C., 45, 47
Lord, John King, 9
Lysaught Report, 113

Male students, Mary Hitchcock Memorial Hospital School of Nursing, 120
Mary Hitchcock Memorial Hospital, 9, 16, 17, 18, 24, 29, 30, 32, 34, 35, 38, 43, 44, 46, 47, 48, 52, 56, 62, 63, 67, 68, 69, 74, 78, 79, 80, 82, 86, 87, 96, 97, 101, 102, 103, 105, 106, 107, 110, 113 illus., 115, 116, 119, 121, 124, 125
Mary Hitchcock Memorial Hospital School of Anesthesia Technology, 80
Mary Hitchcock Memorial Hospital School of Nursing, 50, 51, 62, 64, 65, 66, 69, 70, 74, 80, 81, 82, 83, 84, 86, 97, 100, 101, 102, 104, 108, 110, 117, 120, 127, 130
Mary Hitchcock Memorial Hospital Training School for Nurses, 3, 9, 14, 16, 19, 21, 26 illus., 31, 32, 45, 46, 48, 50
"Mary's House," 51, 56
McGinley, Clair E., 117
McGrath, Marion, 117
McLane, John, 29
McLeod, Jeannie, 141
Medical Nursing, 13, 57, 101
Medical science, 1, 2, 7, 17, 41, 75, 112
Metcalf, Laura M., 141
Military nursing, 33, 75, 76, 92
Montag, Dr. Mildred, 93
Morey, Ada J., 29
Moss and Hunt Aptitude Test for Nursing, 66
Muzzy, Harriet Spaulding, 141

Nathan Smith Laboratory of Dartmouth College, 22
National Commission for the Study of Nursing and Nursing Education in the United States, 113
National League for Nursing, 92, 94, 100, 103, 113, 121, 123, 124, 129
National League of Nursing Education, 28, 42, 48, 61, 64, 68
National Organization of Public Health Nurses, 42
NLN Board of Review for Diploma Programs, 103
NLNE Curriculum Guide, 61, 62, 68
National Nursing Council for War, 76
National Student Nurses' Association, 114
Navy Nurse Corps, 33, 75
Newspaper, school of nursing, 86, 87

New York, early center of nursing affairs, 28
Night duty, 12, 24, 25, 57, 71, 72
Nightengale, Florence, 2 fn.
Nightengale plan, 2
Near East Commission, 37
New Hampshire Board of Nursing Education and Nurse Registration, 94, 123, 129
New Hampshire State Board of Nurse Examiners, 30, 32, 36, 64, 94, 99
New Hampshire Department of Public Instruction, 32
New Hampshire Hospital, 81, 82, 86, 103, 105
New Hampshire League for Nursing, 69
New Hampshire Legislature, 29
New Hampshire Nurses Association, 31, 95
New Hampshire State Board of Education, 48, 58, 68
New Hampshire State Board of Nursing, 49, 68
New Hampshire State Hospital for the Insane, 22
New Hampshire Student Nurses' Association, 114 fn.
Norris Cotton Cancer Center, 115
Norton, Max, 82
Nurse Registration, N.H., 30, 94, 95
Nurse Practice Act, N.H., 29, 32, 95
Nurse Practice Act, N.Y., 95
Nurse Training Act of 1964, 93
Nurses' Associated Alumnae of the United States and Canada, 28, 29
Nurses' Coalition for Action In Politics, 114
Nursing Council on National Defense, 80
Nursing practice, 11, 12, 13, 23, 24, 53, 71, 72, 113
Nursing supervisors, 23, 24, 47, 57, 73, 99

Obstetrical nursing, 13, 57, 101, 103, 107, 119
Occum Pond, 73
Office of Civilian Defense, 76
Operating room nursing, 14, 24, 25 illus., 58, 72

Patten House, 80, 84
Pediatric Nursing, 19, 57, 58, 67, 101, 103, 107, 119
Personnel department, Mary Hitchcock Memorial Hospital, 127
Pike House, 21, 43 illus., 45
Pike, Mrs. A. A., 21
Pilgrims, 1
Practical nurse, 78
Preliminary term 11, 70, 71
Primary nursing, 113, 116
Principal, School of Nursing, 68, 78, 81, 82, 85
Private duty nursing, 13, 26, 48, 61, 63, 72
Probationary period, 11, 11 fn., 24, 25, 52, 53, 84
Proctors, 121
Prohibition, 41
Prouty, Marilyn P., 115, 116, 117, 117 fn., 124, 125, 126
Psychiatric nursing, 49, 81, 82, 86, 92, 103, 105, 119
Public health, 41, 42
Public Health nursing, 42, 48
Public Health Service, 76

Raven, Professor Anton A., 79
Recruitment, school of nursing, 97, 99, 100, 120
Red Cross Nursing Service, 33, 36
Registrar, school of nursing, 120
Robbins, Christie W., 141
Rockefeller Foundation, 42
Roosevelt, Franklin D., 76
Rules/regulations, school of nursing, 25, 26, 58, 73, 108, 109, 110

Salk polio vaccine, 96
"Salus," 111
Samuel, Edith, 141
Sanger, Margaret H., 42 fn.
Schaefer, Cecilia, 78
Schenk, Katherine, 96, 102, 103, 105, 117
Schmidt, Louise M., 141
School of Nursing Advisory Committee, 99, 124
Senior Girl Scouts, 80
Senior Privileges, 109

Senior Sister, 70, 84
Shearman, Caroline, 117 fn.
Shepard, Ida Frances, 15, 16, 29, 30, 31, 32, 37, 45, 46, 47, 51
Smith, Donald S., 63, 78
Smith, Dr. William T., 14
Snell, Edna B., 30
Social Security Act, 61
Spanish American War, 33
Special Care Unit, 96
Staff nurses, 69, 99
State Board Examinations, 30, 92, 93
State Board Examination Test Pool, 92
State Relief of New Hampshire, 63
Statewide Interdisciplinary Planning Project for Nursing and Nursing Education, 115
Straw, Alice, 96, 115, 116, 117, 123
Student activities, 26, 31, 56, 58, 59, 73, 86, 87, 110, 111
Student Bill of Rights, 121
Student government, 87, 108, 110, 121
Student health program, 66, 105, 106, 121, 127
Superintendent, Mary Hitchcock Memorial Hospital, 9, 11, 12, 15, 16, 21 illus., 23, 23 illus., 24, 29, 32, 37, 45, 46, 63, 65, 68, 78
Superintendent of Nurses, 45, 47, 64, 67, 67 illus., 68, 69, 73, 74, 78, 81, 82, 83
Superintendent of Public Instruction, 29
Surgical nursing, 13, 24, 57, 101
Suture nurses, 99

Taft-Hartley Act, 114
Team nursing, 78, 97, 116
Temporary Accrediting Service, NLN, 92
Trustees, Mary Hitchcock Memorial Hospital, 19, 21, 22, 78, 125

Uniform, school of nursing, 11, 20 illus., 53, 70, 87, 98 illus., 116 illus.
United States Cadet Nurse Corps., 76, 77, 79, 81 illus., 82, 84, 87
United States Congress, 75, 76
University System of New Hampshire, 118 fn.

Varnum, James W., 117
Victory Garden, School of Nursing, 86
Volunteers, 79, 80, 82, 85

Walker, Bertha L., 141
Ward, Elizabeth Bowles, 96
West Ward, 19, 62, 69
Williams, Nellie Sweet, 141
Winifred S. Raven Convalescent Unit, 79, 95
Wilson, William L., 78, 95, 117
Womens' Club of Hanover, 22 fn., 44, 46
Women's movement, 41, 114
Wood, Mary Frances, 22 fn.
Works Progress Administration, 61
World War I, 27, 33, 34, 35, 36, 37, 38, 41, 43, 75
World War II, 75, 76, 77, 78, 79, 84, 85, 86, 87, 95

Yearbooks, school of nursing, 111

Zeller, Paul, 111